Strange
Kentucky Monsters

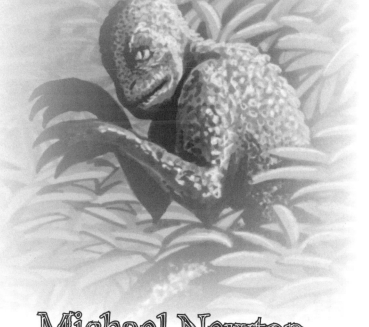

Michael Newton

4880 Lower Valley Road, Atglen, Pennsylvania 19310

Dedication

For Dr. Paul LeBlond

Schiffer Books are available at special discounts for bulk purchases for sales promotions or premiums. Special editions, including personalized covers, corporate imprints, and excerpts can be created in large quantities for special needs. For more information contact the publisher:

Published by Schiffer Publishing Ltd.
4880 Lower Valley Road
Atglen, PA 19310
Phone: (610) 593-1777; Fax: (610) 593-2002
E-mail: Info@schifferbooks.com

For the largest selection of fine reference books on this and related subjects,
please visit our web site at **www.schifferbooks.com**
We are always looking for people to write books on new and related subjects.
If you have an idea for a book please contact us at the above address.

This book may be purchased from the publisher.
Include $5.00 for shipping.
Please try your bookstore first.
You may write for a free catalog.

In Europe, Schiffer books are distributed by
Bushwood Books
6 Marksbury Ave.
Kew Gardens
Surrey TW9 4JF England
Phone: 44 (0) 20 8392-8585; Fax: 44 (0) 20 8392-9876
E-mail: info@bushwoodbooks.co.uk
Website: www.bushwoodbooks.co.uk

Text by Michael Newton
Photos courtesy by author unless otherwise noted.
Artwork by William M. Rebsamen

Copyright © 2010 by Michael Newton
Library of Congress Control Number: 2009940051

Designed by Mark David Bowyer
Type set in !SketchyTimes / New Baskerville BT

ISBN: 978-0-7643-3440-5
Printed in the United States of America

Contents

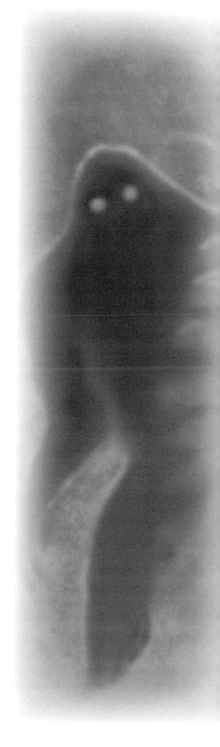

Acknowledgments

I owe thanks to the following individuals, without whom *Strange Kentucky Monsters* would not exist: David Frasier at Indiana University for his usual masterful work in retrieving obscure information; Pamela Platt at the *Louisville Courier-Journal*; Ray Crowe, founder of the International Bigfoot Society; Robert Luginbill and Mary Makris at the University of Louisville; Graham Troop at the Oldham County Library; John Lutz, founding director of the Eastern Puma Research Network; Lee McClellan and Keith Wethington, information officers with the Kentucky Department of Fish and Wildlife Resources; Bob Hahn, librarian for the *Cincinnati Post*; Rhonda Burks at the Mahan-Oldham County Library; Nancy Theiss, executive director of the Oldham County Historical Society; Ann Harding at the Campbell County Public Library, Fort Thomas branch; Mary Adams, director of the Dawson Springs Branch Library; Nancy Shewmaker at the Bullitt County Library in Shepherdsville; Dr. Paul LeBlond; Dr. Karl Shuker; Mary Jane Nelson; Jewell Castle; Bill Rebsamen, for his peerless illustrations; and to my wife Heather, for kind assistance and keen criticism at each phase of the project's development. Finally, to Laura Sutton at UPK for trying her best, and to Dinah Roseberry at Schiffer Books, for an eleventh-hour save.

01.
Kentucky's counties. *Image Courtesy of U.S. Census Bureau*

Introduction

People love monsters. The mythology of every race and culture teems with dragons, giants, shape-shifters, vampires, and weird human-animal hybrids. In the endless struggle between good and evil, light and dark, some aid humanity while others scheme against us; others yet are neutral, only intervening in the cosmic show for personal amusement.[1]

Few classic monsters managed to survive the Age of Reason, though a handful—demons, vampires, werewolves, zombies—cling to life (or un-death) with a helping hand from Hollywood. We still love monsters from a distance, safely trapped within the confines of a novel, theater, or television screen. It is a very different story, though, when they emerge as flesh and blood, prowling our forests, paddling in our lakes and rivers, lurching through our own backyards. The fascination lingers, but its thrill is tinged with fear.

In modern times the "monster" label is applied to creatures great and small that have avoided recognition by the representatives of mainstream science. And, despite prevailing sentiment that Earth has been both thoroughly explored and overrun by legions of humanity, such creatures still appear with striking regularity on every continent except Antarctica, in every sea and ocean of the world.

In 1812, French zoologist Georges Cuvier, renowned as the "father of paleontology," declared, "There is little hope of discovering new species of large quadrupeds." As for reported sea monsters, he wrote, "I hope nobody will ever seriously look for them in nature; one could as well search for the animals of Daniel or the beast of the Apocalypse." Cuvier lived long enough to see himself proved wrong with the discovery of the American tapir (1819) and the whale shark (1828), but he never learned the true scope of his error.[2]

In fact, despite Cuvier's rash prediction, new species were uncovered at a rate of 4,500 per year throughout the Nineteenth Century, expanding to 12,000 per year in the first half of the Twentieth Century, and seldom dipped below 9,000 per year after 1950. Granted, most of those species ranged from relatively small in size to microscopic, but large surprises still awaited searchers. They included the lowland gorilla (1847), the pygmy hippopotamus (1870), Cotton's white rhinoceros (1900), the okapi (1901), the mountain gorilla (1902), the giant forest hog (1904), Dawson's caribou (1908), the Komodo dragon (1912), the kouprey (1937), the saola (1992), the giant muntjac (1997), and the leaf muntjac (1997). At sea, discoveries undreamed by Cuvier include sixteen species of whales (1823-1913), the whale shark (1828), the giant squid (1857), living coelacanths (1938), and the megamouth shark (1976). Scientific estimates of species still unknown today range from two million to twenty million or more. Frederick Grassle, director of Rutgers University's Institute of Marine and Coastal Sciences, estimates that the deep sea alone may conceal ten million species from humanity's prying eyes.[3]

02.
Two surprise discoveries from the Twentieth Century: Africa's okapi (left) and the giant muntjac. *Artwork Courtesy of William Rebsamen*

While most "new" creatures and the vast majority of those as yet unknown are no more monstrous than the average dog or deer, a few described by witnesses are large and frightening enough to keep the monster label firmly established in popular usage. So it doubtless shall remain, and I employ the term in this work without the slightest malice toward whatever creatures share our planet in the modern age.

Tireless researcher Chad Arment has classified the creatures normally pursued by cryptozoologists—seekers of "hidden" or "unexpected" animals—into four broad categories that are helpful in our effort to bring order out of fragmentary and sometimes chaotic eyewitness reports. Those groups include:

(1) Animals similar to known living species, but with phenotypic differences (such as spotted lions or eighty-foot pythons).

(2) Animals similar to known living species, sighted far outside their normal range (such as "black panthers" prowling North America).

(3) Animals resembling members of species presumed to be extinct worldwide or extirpated in a given area (such as living dinosaurs in Africa or cougars dwelling east of the Mississippi River).

(4) Animals apparently unrelated to any known species, living or extinct (including giant apes at large in the United States).[4]

Any list of Earth's most famous unknown creatures would include the Himalayan Yeti, Scotland's Nessie, and Bigfoot, but would-be cryptozoologists need not spend a fortune on travel to Asia, Britain, or the Pacific Northwest. In fact, most need to look no farther then the nearest swamp or woodland.

Strange Kentucky Monsters is the first dedicated book-length survey of anomalous fauna in the Bluegrass State. Previous works, from Paul Atkinson's *Kentucky, Land of Legend and Lore* (1962) to Barton Nunnelly's *Mysterious Kentucky* (2007), examine various unknown creatures in combination with aboriginal folklore, hauntings, UFOs, and human oddities.

Strange Kentucky Monsters consists of six chapters, topically arranged.

Chapter 1 examines Kentucky's known exotic or invasive species, together with some presently unrecognized by state wildlife authorities.

Chapter 2 presents case histories of alien big cats reported statewide.

Chapter 3 surveys reports of giant unidentified reptiles spanning 118 years of Kentucky history.

Chapter 4 pursues Kentucky's lake and river monsters.

Chapter 5 explores the state's long history of unknown primate sightings, describing a creature best known as Bigfoot or Sasquatch.

Chapter 6 comprises a menagerie of creatures fitting none of the previous categories.

The conclusion surveys Kentucky's mountains, forests, lakes, and swamps as potential monster havens in the new millennium.

1.
Hypothetical Inhabitants

Kentucky's Department of Fish and Wildlife Resources (DFWR) recognizes 1,087 species of animals presently living within the Bluegrass State. Insects, excluded from the wildlife list, add more than 10,000 species to Kentucky's diverse faunal roster. Curiously, while the Kentucky Exotic Pest Plant Council maintains a list of ninety-six invasive plant species found in the state, no corresponding list of exotic animal species exists.[1]

Nonetheless, due diligence permits us to create our own list of exotic animals, a tentative field guide to "alien" species. Some are literal aliens, invaders from distant continents; others apparently fell through the cracks when state wildlife biologists prepared their master list of known Kentucky animals. In either case, they are fair game for amateur cryptozoologists.

We begin our search with the smallest, most plentiful creatures of all.

Insects

Insects comprise seventy-five percent of Earth's known animal species. They also represent the largest number of new species classified by scientists in any given year. The twin secrets of their success are prolificacy and wings. Since most insects can fly at some stage in their lives, humans find it nearly impossible to curb their spread around the globe.[2]

Because insects are not considered wildlife, the DFWR does not maintain a list of known Kentucky species. The University of Kentucky's entomology department estimates Kentucky's insect population in excess of 10,000 species, their number augmented by "many different kinds" of arachnids (spiders, scorpions, etc.).[3] The absence of a comprehensive master list frustrates our effort to identify exotic insects in the state, but one invasive species is well known.

The Asian tiger mosquito, or forest day mosquito (*Aedes albopictus*), entered North America aboard a shipment of used auto tires in 1985, at the port of Houston, Texas. Over the next two decades, it spread throughout the southeastern United States, including all of Kentucky, and along the East Coast as far north as Maine. Mosquitoes typically pursue humans, not the reverse, but avid seekers after A. albopictus should be aware that a domestic species, Ochlerotatus canadensis, mimics the Asian tiger's striped legs.[4]

Aquatic Species

Kentucky's DFWR recognizes 538 living species of aquatic animals, including 208 mollusks, 81 crustaceans, 242 fish, and 7 lampreys. Four of those species are invasive exotics, while a fifth may lurk in Bluegrass waters, as yet unobserved.[5]

Kentucky's smallest exotic water-dweller is the zebra mussel (*Dreissena polymorpha*), a Eurasian species that entered North America through the Great Lakes in 1988 and subsequently spread along major rivers. Adult females produce between 30,000 and 400,000 eggs per year, thereby accounting for the zebra's rapid advance. Zebra mussels disrupt the ecosystem by starving out native species, while damaging boats, harbors, and power plants. Kentucky wildlife authorities acknowledge only seven zebra mussel sightings in the state—six undated reports from Marshall County, and one from Carlisle County in October 1997—but federal sources disagree. An online map prepared by the U.S. Fish and Wildlife Service depicts zebra mussel infestations bisecting the state from Boone and Kenton Counties southward to Lake Cumberland, while other colonies crowd the Ohio and Tennessee Rivers in western Kentucky.[6]

Three species of Asian carp comprise the remainder of Kentucky's acknowledged exotic fish species. First to arrive was the grass carp or white amur (*Ctenopharyngodon idella*), a herbivorous fish deliberately introduced to the United States in 1963 for aquatic weed control. Since then, it has proliferated, recognized by DFWR spokesmen from fourteen reports in twelve Kentucky counties between 1983 and 2000. Counties affected include Ballard, Breckinridge, Carlisle, Crittenden, Fulton, Hickman, Jefferson, Letcher, Mason, Montgomery, Shelby, and Trigg. The true extent of grass carp infestation may only be surmised.[7]

Two other species of Asian carp, the closely related bighead carp (*Hypophthalmichthys nobilis*) and silver carp (*H. molitrix*), also inhabit Kentucky waters. Both were imported during the 1970s, to control algae and plankton growth in aquaculture and municipal wastewater treatment facilities, and both escaped to breed in the wild. The DFWR lists bigheads among Kentucky's fish, while strangely reporting that "no county record was found" for any specimens. Two undated sightings of silver carp in Jefferson and Union Counties complete the state's census.

Federal authorities began work on a plan to control Asian carp in April 2007, with no deadline announced for final action.[8]

03.
A bighead carp caught in American waters.
Image Courtesy of U.S. Fish & Wildlife Service

The most fearsome potential invader of Kentucky's lakes and rivers remains at this writing a hypothetical menace. The northern snakehead (*Channa argus*), a freshwater native of Russia, China, and Korea, is an obligate air breather, possessing an unusual respiratory system that allows it to live outside of water for several days at a time. Young specimens may even travel overland for short distances, though Chinese researchers insist that adults lose that skill. The snakehead's striking appearance, voracious appetite, and reputation for straying ashore make it an ideal subject for horror fiction, including four Hollywood films released between 2003 and 2006.[9]

04.
Asian snakehead fish have invaded U.S. waterways. *Image Courtesy of U.S. Fish & Wildlife Service*

According to the U.S. Fish and Wildlife Service, 16,554 live snakeheads were imported into the United States between 1997 and 2000. A Maryland fisherman hooked the first wild specimen in 2002, prompting an official counterattack that swept two adult snakeheads and more than 100 juvenile specimens from the Chesapeake watershed. By 2006, snakeheads had been pulled from lakes and rivers in thirteen states, ranging from Washington and California to New England, Florida, and Texas.[10]

Kentucky has thus far escaped infestation, joining twelve other states that ban importation or possession of snakeheads, but the strange invaders may be on their way. In May 2005, DFWR agents seized a live snakehead from the Hopkins County home of Brian Dunbar, who purchased the fish from a Tennessee pet store. That infraction cost Dunbar a $25 fine plus court costs, but the risk of apprehension is slight. Federal authorities note that the trend in snakehead imports "has been toward an increase in recent years." Live specimens are sold in Boston and New York fish markets, and also on the Internet.[11]

Amphibians

Kentucky wildlife officers acknowledge fifty-four species of amphibians living statewide. They include thirty-four salamanders and twenty frogs or toads.[12] However, consultation with the standard field guide reveals at least nine species or subspecies recognized by herpetologists that stand excluded from the DFWR's master list.

Five salamanders somehow failed to make the cut. State biologists acknowledge the presence of eastern newts (*Notophthalmus viridescens*), but fail to distinguish its two Kentucky-dwelling subspecies. One, the red-spotted newt (*N. v. viridescens*) grows to nearly five inches in length and inhabits three-fourths of the state, excluding far-western Kentucky. There, its place is taken by the central newt (*N. v. louisianaensis*), which does not exceed four inches overall and generally shows no spots.[13]

Kentucky's other "missing" salamanders include the eastern zigzag salamander (*Plethodon dorsalis dorsalis*), the Mississippi slimy salamander (*P. Mississippi*), and the northern spring salamander (*Gyrinophilus porphyristicus porphyristicus*). In the latter case, state agents list a different subspecies, the Kentucky spring salamander (*G. p. duryi*), whose record length is a full inch shorter than the 7.5 inches recorded for *G. p. porphyristicus*.[14]

The state's census of living amphibians also omits three subspecies of frogs and toads. They include Blanchard's cricket frog (*Acris crepitans blanchardi*), the bronze frog (*Rana clamitans clamitans*), and the dwarf American toad (*Bufo americanus charlesmithi*). In each case, the DFWR lists different species that also inhabit Kentucky. Omission of recognized subspecies may be intended to simplify the state's list, but do take note that there are some species missing.[15]

Reptiles

A similar issue arises in our survey of KY reptiles. The DFWR lists fifty-seven reptile species on its roster, fifteen turtles, eight lizards, and thirty-four snakes.[16] Consultation of a standard field guide reveals no fewer than twenty species or subspecies missing from the official census.

Three Kentucky-dwelling turtles find no place on the DFWR's list. They include the eastern river cooter (*Pseudemys concinna concinna*) and the hieroglyphic river cooter (*P. c. hieroglyphica*), both from the far-western counties; and the midland painted turtle (*Chrysemys picta marginata*), found statewide.[17]

The state's reporting of northern coal skinks (*Eumeces anthracinus anthracinus*) with a southern subspecies (*E. a. pluvialis*) may be simple shorthand, since the list includes a coal skink without reference to subspecies. In fact, however, both lizards inhabit different parts of Kentucky. Examination of the supralabial (upper lip) scales may be required to distinguish the subspecies.[18]

Fifteen snake subspecies should be added to the state list as well. They include the midland water snake (*Nerodia sipedon pleuralis*) and the yellow-belly water snake (*N. erythrogaster flavigaster*); the northern brown snake (*Storeria dekayi dekayi*) and the midland brown snake (*S. d. wrightorum*); the northern ringneck (*Diadophis punctatus edwardsii*) and the Mississippi ringneck (*D. p. stictogenys*); the eastern worm snake (*Carphophis amoenus amoenus*) and the Midwest worm snake (*C. a. helenae*); the northern black racer (*Coluber constrictor constrictor*) and southern black racer (*C. c. priapus*); the gray rat snake (*Elaphe obsoleta spilodes*); the eastern milk snake (*Lampropeltis triangulum triangulum*) and red milk snake (*L. t. syspila*); the northern copperhead (*Agkistrodon contortix mokasen*) and the southern copperhead (*A. c. contortix*). Again, while the state's roster includes some general species listings, omission of so many subspecies is inconsistent with the DFWR's treatment of other animals in the same document. Again, the state's roster includes some general species listings but their are omissions of subspecies for you to look into. As a note, other animals in the same state document seem to be well-researched.[19]

A more startling snake tale emerged from Paducah on May 24, 2006, when Dan McBride, assistant athletic director at Eastern Kentucky University, found a two-foot-long ball python (*Python regius*) coiled inside his rented car. Ball pythons, while native to Africa, are frequently sold as pets in the United States. Paducah authorities presume the snake had escaped from captivity, but at last report, the supposed negligent owner remained unidentified.[20]

05.
An American alligator.
*Image Courtesy of U.S.
Fish & Wildlife Service*

American alligators (*Alligator mississippiensis*) are not native to Kentucky, but they find their way into the Bluegrass State from time to time. As with large exotic snakes, authorities normally blame careless pet owners for importing gators, though the human culprits are rarely discovered. In May 2007, DFWR agents charged Stephanie Osborn, owner of a Pike County pet shop, with illegally transporting a juvenile alligator, but charges were dismissed after she euthanized the reptile. Outlaw gator-wranglers remain unidentified in Oak Grove, where a 4.5-foot alligator was recovered from the basement of an abandoned house in September 2005, and in Maysville, where a three-foot specimen emerged from a garbage dumpster in December 2006. The case of "Captain Chaos"—a three-foot gator pulled from the Kentucky River near Winchester's Clays Ferry dock—is less certain. Mark Gumbert, a Kentucky Power biologist, caught the alligator on July 3, 2001, and subsequently arranged for its relocation to South Carolina.[21]

Birds

Kentucky DFWR spokesmen recognize 363 species of birds living wild in Kentucky. One, the European starling (*Sturnus vulgaris*), is a bona fide exotic, introduced to the United States from Eurasia circa 1890-91. We owe their importation to Eugene Schieffelin, head of a New York City "acclimatization society" bent on introducing every bird species mentioned in the works of William Shakespeare. From Schieffelin's original sixty birds, released in Central Park, an estimated 200 million European starlings now infest North America, including all 120 Kentucky counties. They drive out native species and appropriate their nests, thereby disrupting the natural order from coast to coast.[22]

Ornithologists also recognize two additional species to be added to the DFWR listing. The common snipe (*Gallinago gallinago*) is a year-round resident statewide, but does not rate inclusion on the master list. A more unusual visitor, the band-rumped storm-petrel (*Oceanodroma castro*), is a tropical island-dweller that follows the Gulf Stream along the Eastern Seaboard from May to late August, and should have no business in Kentucky. Nonetheless, the Kentucky Ornithological Society lists O. castro as a species documented from the Bluegrass State "with specimens and/or photographs."[23]

Mammals

Kentucky officially claims seventy-one mammal species, but there's another species to be added according to the U.S. Department of Agriculture, or Bluegrass hunting guides who advertise boar-hunting safaris online. Wild boars (*Sus scrofa*) are natives of Eurasia, imported to the West Indies by Christopher Columbus in 1493, and on to the North American mainland by various sixteenth-century explorers. Today they roam free in at least twenty-six states. [24]

06.
A typical wild boar. *Image Courtesy of U.S. Fish & Wildlife Service*

While wild boars go officially unrecognized in Kentucky, their kin in other states reach truly monstrous sizes. A specimen dubbed "Hogzilla," 8 feet long and weighing 800 pounds, was shot by a Georgia hunter in June 2004. A second Georgia hog, killed in January 2007, tipped the scales at 1,100 pounds. Another porcine behemoth, allegedly 9 feet four inches long and weighing 1,051 pounds, died at the hands of an Alabama hunter in May 2007.[25] No specimens approaching that size have yet been found in Kentucky, but the mere possibility may give hunters pause.

Primates

Homo sapiens are the sole recognized North American primate. Only in Florida, where wildlife authorities grant the existence of three monkey species breeding in the wild since 1930, are exotic primate colonies officially acknowledged.[26] Still, reports of apes or monkeys at large persist from many other states, with Kentucky no exception.

And what stories they are!

The first report emerged from Jessamine County in 1831. Witness Patrick Flournoy, while descending a cliff on the north bank of the Kentucky River, was startled to see a "one-eyed ape" lounging beneath a nearby tree, its stout tail wrapped around a low-hanging branch. At sight of Flournoy, the creature scrambled up into the branches and was lost to sight. Flournoy described its single eye as white and silver dollar-sized, set in the middle of the ape's forehead.[27]

Kentucky's next encounter with a large, long-tailed primate occurred in April 1944, but no report of the event was published until 1978. That December, Shirley Elkins of Paintsville, in Johnson County, wrote to the New England Bigfoot Information Center, describing her experience as a night-shift nurse at an unnamed hospital. According to Elkins, a man checked in with "a mess of scratches" which he declined to explain. Nurse Elkins married her patient in June 1945, only then hearing his strange tale of assault in the woods by a man-sized primate with "aqua-colored eyes," slate-gray fur, and a long bushy tail. The beast snarled, mauled its victim, then fled with some catfish he was cleaning. It left "five-toed tracks...that had the impression of claws."[28]

Twenty-nine years after the Paintsville incident, in autumn 1973, three large and violent primates visited Trimble County, on the Ohio River. Albany farmer Charlie Stern watched a six-foot-tall beast with "an ape-human face and a bushy black tail" kill one of his animals, then fired multiple close-range gunshots without any visible effect. After standing its ground in a hail of bullets, the creature finally fled, running upright on two legs. Other local witnesses described two large apes traveling in company with a smaller "young one." Author Loren Coleman toured the area and found strange three-toed tracks at the site of one encounter.[29]

07.
Witnesses report encounters with unknown primates resembling baboons. *Image Courtesy of U.S. National Oceanic and Atmospheric Administration*

Coleman, collaborating with fellow researchers Chad Arment and Mark Hall, hypothesizes the existence of an unclassified North American primate species, which he dubs "devil monkeys." Various reports, ranging from British Columbia to Virginia, describe barrel-chested primates four to six feet tall, with long tails and doglike faces reminiscent of a baboon's. Their footprints measure twelve to fifteen inches long and frequently display three toes, unlike those of the Paintsville beast. Coleman goes further yet, suggesting that large devil monkeys may account for some reports of kangaroos at large in the United States.[30]

It has been noted that, though there have been several reliable sightings, the DFWR spokespeople reject the possibility of devil monkeys prowling through Kentucky's woods.

2.
Alien Big Cats

In strict scientific terms, "big cats" (or "great cats") are members of the genus Panthera, including the jaguar, leopard, lion, and tiger. All are distinguished by their specially adapted larynx and hyoid apparatus, which enables them to roar but restricts their ability to purr. A broader definition based on size treats cougars, cheetahs, clouded leopards, and snow leopards as big cats. A further distinction involves the labeling of offspring, known as "cubs" for big cats and as "kittens" for all other feline species.[1]

The label "alien big cat" (or "ABC") is commonly applied by cryptozoologists to any of the cats listed above, when they are found in the wild, outside their normal range. African cats are "alien" when found roaming at large on any other continent. Cougars and jaguars are deemed alien when found outside of the Americas or living wild in areas from which they have been extirpated and are deemed officially extinct.[2]

Phantom Cougars

The cougar (*Puma concolor*)—also known as mountain lion, panther, and puma—is the New World's second-largest cat, after the jaguar, and ranks as the fourth-largest felid on Earth. Science recognized thirty-two cougar subspecies until the latter 1990s, when study of mitochondrial DNA reduced the tally to six. Five subspecies are confined to Latin America, while the sixth (*P. c. cougar*) now includes seventeen obsolete subspecies found throughout Canada, the United States, and Mexico.[3]

Cougars once ranged throughout North America, from coast to coast, but a war of attrition by hunters and settlers allegedly exterminated all big cats east of the Mississippi River by the early Twentieth Century. No official date is available for the death of Kentucky's last cougar, but authors Roger Barbour and Wayne Davis, in their Mammals of Kentucky

(1974), found "no valid records [of wild cougars] for some 75 years"— i.e., since 1899. Other reports suggest that cougars were annihilated in the 1850s. Today, Kentucky's Department of Fish and Wildlife Resources considers cougars extirpated from the state, and private ownership is banned by law. State spokesmen generally agree with Barbour and Davis that modern sightings of cougars "are probably based on escaped animals or a vivid imagination."[4]

And yet, cougars refuse to vanish from the Bluegrass State. A specimen was killed and photographed at Central City (Muhlenberg County) in 1960, and while rumors suggested that it had escaped from a roadside zoo, that claim was never proven. The Eastern Puma Research Network's files contain ninety-eight cougar sightings logged between 1965 and 2005, including eight cases where adult cats were seen with cubs. John Lutz, the network's founder and director, further reports that on some unspecified occasion "tracks of a cougar were found and identified by a state forester, but were later denied by a Kentucky Wildlife Conservation Officer."[5]

The DFWR logged another spate of cougar sightings in the 1970s. Forest Douthitt, a Henry County farmer, met a cougar on his property in summer 1976. Neighbor Frank Dale saw the same cat or its twin a few months later, while hunting along the Kentucky River. Despite the escalating number of reports, state spokesmen remained skeptical. In July 1980, DFWR biologist Chester Stephens told *Louisville Courier-Journal* columnist Byron Crawford, "The only report I've had that I feel right about came from Menifee County in '78. Two loggers on a log road said they saw a large, long-tailed cat jump out in the road in front of them and run up the road about 200 yards."[6]

In autumn 1979, the DFWR conducted the state's first-ever census of mammals, planting scent posts at 300 scattered locations statewide, then recording the animal tracks found nearby. Robert Morton, a state biologist operating from Hazard, found a cat's paw print 3 inches long and 3.5 inches wide near a scent post on Pine Mountain, southwest of Whitesburg, but he stopped short of declaring it a cougar track. "We've found bobcat tracks 2½ inches wide and 2 inches long," Morton told Byron Crawford, "and the only foolproof way to identify the species' track is to see him standing in it, then take four different photographs of him."[7]

Barbara Rosenman, a former DFWR employee who now serves as director of Oldham County Animal Control, graciously shared her files of "weird sightings" for use in this book. Those files include DFWR internal memos of cougar sightings reported between 1986 and 1996. The memos document a consistent series of cougar sightings.

08.
Cougars continue to appear in areas where they are said to be extinct.
Image Courtesy of U.S. Fish & Wildlife Service

Witness Blaine Cravens waited a decade to report his 1986 sighting near Orville, along the Kentucky River in Henry County. Cravens was bow hunting on a relative's farm when he saw a cougar and spent ten minutes watching it. He later described the cat as tan, weighing approximately ninety pounds, with a long tail.[8]

On May 1, 1989, the DFWR received a report from Borowick Farms, in Oldham County. The cat seen there had "brownish gray fur with [a] broken spotted pattern of dark gray, [a] long tail, bushy, with stripes and black tip." The unnamed witness noted facial ruffs and remarked on the cat's "leaping gait." The animal stood roughly thirty inches tall at the shoulder and appeared to be three feet long from its nose to the base of its tail.[9]

Prospect resident John Lutzon saw an apparent cougar near his home on November 9, 1990. He reported the sighting, whereupon a DFWR agent advised him "to look at the animal's tracks and check for claw prints," which might indicate that he had seen a dog. No record exists of any further investigation.[10]

Stacy Damrel, a deliveryman for the *Richmond Register*, was making his rounds at 4 a.m. on October 19, 1991, when he heard screams like a child's on Darlene Court, off Tates Creek Road. Damrel had just returned to his truck from dropping a bundle of papers and turned on his headlights, to find a cougar lounging in front of the vehicle. "At first he was laying down," Damrel said, "but he stood up when I turned my lights on and started pacing back and forth."[11]

Damrel fled but reported the sighting, which prompted local outdoorsman Tom Powell to recount his own experience from years past. His dogs had treed a cougar, Powell told the *Register*, but he refused to shoot it. "I called off the dogs and he came down the tree a few feet," Powell recalled. "He was twenty feet in the air and he just jumped down and ran off. I've heard stories about them since I was a boy, of people seeing them all the time. People have seen them for years and years and everybody thought we were crazy."[12]

In the predawn hours of October 15, 1993, a cougar attacked one of Patricia Keen's dogs at her farm outside Burkesville, in Cumberland County. Mrs. Keen shouted at the cat, then ran to fetch her gun, but the cougar fled, trailed by two cubs the size of Keen's Labrador retriever. The adult cat, she guessed, had been 7 feet long, including its tail. Son Brian Keen, a zoology student at Western Kentucky University, made a plaster cast of the cougar's paw print, measuring 4.5 inches wide.[13]

Marcus Cope, a government biologist employed at Land Between the Lakes National Recreation Area (LBL), prepared a summary of local cougar sightings on February 9, 1994. It reads, in part: "LBL has one plaster cast of a cougar track made on their grounds. Look at a map showing areas where deer were never exterminated in Kentucky and those are the areas where cougar sightings have persisted....A fellow in Calloway County had many large captive predators, including cougars. This is not far from LBL....A [DFWR] employee... doing turkey research at LBL spotted a cougar using binoc[ular]s. Considered a most reliable sighting. Kentucky's cats COULD BE remnants of the historical population, could be Westerns moving their range eastward, most likely are released captives. Could be exotic cats. Could be a combination of the above."[14]

On April 11, 1994, witness Wanda McCallister reported a cougar sighting from her Louisville home in Sandstone Estates, on Rough River Lake (Grayson County). It marked her second meeting with a cougar in five years. The cat was limping, she said, and appeared to be injured. Officer Gerry Rau denied McCallister permission to shoot the cat if it returned.[15]

Taylorville resident Phil Hawkins saw a cougar prowling around his backyard pond on September 26, 1995. He caught the cat on videotape but the footage has never been aired publicly. Officer Gerry Rau referred Hawkins to another DFWR employee, David McChesnay, and the rest is silence.[16]

Eric Ables, residing on Roy Lane in Lebanon Junction (Bullitt County), heard a "panther" shrieking on his property in November 1995, and subsequently found "tracks from a big cat" in a muddy creek bed. Without investigating at the scene, an unnamed DFWR employee noted the sighting and closed the case with the observation that "I feel it was likely a bobcat."[17]

Two weeks later, on December 5, Harrodsburg heating contractor George Edger saw a cougar on Old Brownstown Road, in Mercer County. The resultant DFWR memo noted that Edger "has photos of the tracks," but they remain unpublished.[18]

Authorities could not ignore the eight-pound female cougar cub struck and killed by a motorist on Route 850, in Floyd County, in June 1997. The driver stopped and saw two other cats retreating from the scene, an adult and another cub the same size as its fallen sibling. Examination of the dead cub revealed that its claws were intact, and that it had no tags or tattoos suggesting prior captivity. Subsequent DNA testing traced its maternal ancestry to a South American cougar subspecies, while its paternal ancestors were North American P. c. cougar. The interbreeding mystery remains unsolved.[19]

Cougar sightings continue across Kentucky in the Twenty-first Century. Witness Bob Craven of Calloway County reports five separate meetings with cougars between September 2000 and November 2004, including two on Blood River Road, two more on Buffalo Road, and one on River Oaks Lane. Craven says that their color ranged "from brownish gray to a dark possibly brown-black color."[20]

In April 2003, Bob Haas and Linda Linde noticed that their dog and four cats had begun to avoid the woods near their Villa Hills home in Kenton County. They soon found a pile of apparent cat droppings, five or six times the size of their dog's normal scat, but thought no more of it until May, when Linde tried moonlight gardening as a cure for insomnia. Frightened by sudden snarls and screeching from the forest, she fled indoors, but the prowler remained invisible. Haas finally saw the cougar in August and reported it to Kenton County Animal Control Officer Junior Creekmore. Despite similar sightings from four other locals since February, Creekmore deemed the encounters "inconclusive." As he explained to the *Cincinnati Post*, "People have told me that they have seen these animals chasing dogs and baby deer. But we've not had any pets I know of attacked."[21]

Bill Reichling, a Kentucky volunteer with the Eastern Puma Research Network, told the *Post* that he had logged seventy-seven cougar sightings—including three of his own—since 1988. "I know we have some transient [cougars] checking out the territory," Reichling said. "We've had too many sightings. Unfortunately, most of the time people don't know about me [to report cougars]. We don't run around with neon signs saying, 'Look at me, I'm a cougar tracker.'" Jim Lane, a wildlife program coordinator for the DFWR, told the *Post*, "We have evidence of cougars in Kentucky, but most of them are captive-raised or captive-bred. I have not heard of any in Northern Kentucky—and a cougar is a pretty secretive animal. To see one living around Villa Hills, if it's indeed a cougar, there's not a doubt in my mind it's one someone's raised and released or [that] got out."[22]

June 2004 brought cougar sightings from Henry County, coupled with reports of missing pets. Dr. Jann Aaron saw a cougar lounging on a flatbed wagon at her farm, in western Henry County. Neighbor Lynda Clark heard feline shrieking from the nearby woods and found a large cat's paw prints. James Mills of Jericho raised the ante, saying, "We've seen the tracks but we haven't seen the actual lions. There are two of 'em out here somewhere. Last night we went out searching for it. I think it was across the field because the horses were screaming." Henry County's game warden acknowledged 30 calls concerning cougars in the past six months, while Dave Hodge—curator of big cats at the Louisville Zoo—declared, "It's a 99.9-percent likelihood these are captive animals that have gotten loose or were released."[23]

That claim was never proven, as the cats moved on to other hunting grounds that summer. August brought a cougar sighting and photos of large tracks from Millerstown, in Grayson County. A witness who preferred anonymity told the Grayson County *News-Gazette*, "It's no bobcat, because I've caught a glimpse of it a couple times. It has a long, bushy tail, not a short one." DFWR spokesmen Norm Mench opined that "[a]ctual cougar sightings are very rare, but anything is within the realm of the possible. What we need to confirm a sighting like this is a good sharp picture of the animal." Three weeks later, Ava Lacy of Saint Charles (Hopkins County) saw two large cats: the smaller weighed "100 pounds or so" and was reddish-brown, while its companion was "very large and black."[24]

And cougar sightings continue statewide. In June 2006, after three local sightings spanning nine months, officials at Mammoth Cave National Park posted public warnings of cougars at large in western Kentucky. Mike Marraccini, speaking for the DFWR, dismissed the problem, saying, "If it is a cougar, it's probably the only one in the state." Perhaps it was the same cat, then, which surfaced at Camp Springs, in Campbell County, during December 2006 and January 2007. Six witnesses reported cougar sightings in three weeks. One felid took an after-hours stroll around the Campbell County Animal Shelter, observed by multiple witnesses at a nearby business establishment. John Dinnon, head of the Cincinnati Zoo's conservation program, accepted the sightings as genuine and told reporters, "I'm not as surprised as I would have been years ago."[25]

The most recent sighting on file, as this work went to press, was reported from Crittenden County in February 2008, by retired Kentucky forestry worker Floyd Wheeler. Wheeler was out for a drive when he saw the cat, later telling journalist Steve Ford, "It was exactly 3:15 p.m. when I saw the varmint. I'm just as sure about what I saw as I am about telling somebody the difference between a fox squirrel and a gray squirrel. I used to deer hunt in Colorado, so I'd seen them in the wild before, although this is the only one I've ever seen in Kentucky. I watched it for 8 minutes and it raised its head 5 times because it knew we were there. It was only about 70 yards away and I had a good enough look at it I can tell you for certain, if you know what I mean, that it was a female between 80 and 85 pounds. It had also been wounded in the right hip and was bleeding a little. I don't know how it got there, but I know what I saw. I'm 100 percent sure I saw a mountain lion in the wild in Kentucky."[26]

Black Panthers

If relict or re-established cougars no longer evoke great surprise, what of "black panthers?" Before examining the problem, we should note that science recognizes no such animals. The cats commonly called black panthers are melanistic jaguars or leopards, whose typical markings remain visible against their dark coats on close examination. Similarly, albino of leucistic individuals of either species are sometimes called "white panthers." There are no scientifically authenticated cases of melanistic cougars, lions, or tigers.[27]

09.
All known "black panthers" are melanistic jaguars or leopards. *Artwork Courtesy of William Rebsamen*

Kentucky researcher Bart Nunnelly asserts that black ABCs were seen by the state's earliest settlers, but he provides no specifics. John Lutz, of the Eastern Puma Research Network, writes that "panther reports were widespread in western Lee County during the 1950s, then extended northeast into the Red River Gorge area in the late 1950s through the 1960s. Others moved south into Clay County and a second area of Daniel Boone National Forest. Another area of great reports stem from Land Between the Lakes for both black panthers and tawny pumas. These reports have been ongoing since the 1960s." Statewide, the network collected twenty-seven reports of black panthers from 1965 through 2004.[28]

Bart Nunnelly claims two sightings of Kentucky panthers, in 1971 and 1988. The first sighting occurred when he was five years old, outside his home in Reed (Henderson County). He described the jet-black cat as roughly four feet long "from nose to tail." He subsequently heard "the panther's bone-chilling screams many times as a child," but did not glimpse another of the cats until he was twenty-two. While strolling along a creek bed in Stanley (Daviess County) with his two brothers, Nunnelly saw a deer pursued by a large quadruped covered with "brownish-gray matted fur—not hair." He concluded that the creature was a gray wolf (*Canis lupus*), another species listed by the DFWR as extirpated from Kentucky, and he was retreating from that encounter when a panther six to seven feet long barred his path. "We all saw it very clearly," he writes in *Mysterious Kentucky*. "There was absolutely no doubt in anyone's mind as to the identity of the animal."[29]

Meanwhile, according to John Lutz, "From the 1970s through the 1990s black panthers were seen or reported around Lake Cumberland [Russell County] and Dale Hollow Lake," spanning the border between Clinton County, Kentucky, and Clay County, Tennessee. During the same period, researcher Fred Mullen collected reports of black ABCs prowling around Allen County's Barren River Lake. A report from the late 1980s, curiously logged on the Gulf Coast Bigfoot Research Organization's website, describes a sighting from McCreary County. There, young cousins were awakened by "some kind of animal screaming" in the woods near their rural home, and two days later saw a panther "slinking across the road like it was trying to make itself less noticeable. It was solid black and was definitely not a dog....It was young because it was not much bigger than a medium-sized dog. We came to the conclusion that it must have lost its mother." Neighbors subsequently saw the cat crossing a nearby field.[30]

Michigan journalist John Castle's interest in the panther phenomenon led him to collect reports from other states as well, including sightings from Kentucky's Crittenden, Hancock, Livingston, and Marshall Counties logged during the 1970s and 1980s. R.D. Norris, a retired electrician from Calvert City, collected "dozens" of panther reports from Livingston and Marshall Counties during 1974-89. Barbara Rosenman's files contain several DFWR memos on black panther sightings logged in 1993-95, although the first was a mistake: An agency employee at the Ballard Wildlife Management Area reportedly saw a "panther" that proved to be a black Labrador retriever.[31]

Two sightings from 1995 are more convincing. Louisville resident Peggy Montgomery saw a "very large cat" outside her Cooper Chapel Road apartment on March 10, 1995, describing it as German-Shepherd-size and "solid black with very pointed ears and a real long tail." Five months later, on August 16, Margie Ferris saw a panther cross Highway 393 near Harrods Creek, in Jefferson County. It resembled "something you would see in the zoo" and displayed a "bold" attitude, showing no fear of her vehicle. A neighbor subsequently acknowledged seeing the cat, but explained that she "did not tell anyone because she thought they would laugh at her."[32]

The Eastern Puma Research Network logged several panther reports around Pine Mountain (Harlan County) in 1999, while a 2001 report from witness "B.A." in Campbellsville (Taylor County) claimed that "many of the locals had seen a black panther in the hills over the years. They said they had not only seen it, but heard it." Brian Peck was driving on Highway 460 near Ezel (Morgan County) in May 2002, when he saw a panther cross the road "in two leaps." Ava Lacy estimated that her Hopkins County panther, seen twice in September 2004, weighed at least 150 pounds. That same summer, while walking her dog near Herrington Lake (Mercer County), Mary Jane Nelson saw a panther drinking from a flooded roadside ditch. "It was beautiful," she writes. "It lifted its head and looked at us, and for seconds nothing moved....Then it turned and ran around the edge of the woods and then disappeared in them." John Lutz has logged no panther sightings from Kentucky since November 2006, but there is no reason to think the cats have disappeared.[33]

Various explanations are advanced for panther sightings in Kentucky and across America at large. John Lutz believes that they are melanistic cougars, thriving in the wild although unrecognized by science. Michigan researcher John Castle suggests they are black leopards, imported as exotic pets in the 1960s. "I'm inclined to think that some people bought these cubs, which became vicious," he says, "and these people had no compunctions at all about taking them out and releasing them wherever they were." Castle's theory may explain some panther sightings, but its self-imposed parameters do not address sightings before the 1960s—or any from the eighteenth and nineteenth centuries, alluded to by Bart Nunnelly.[34]

Earlier sightings may be explained by a variation on Castle's theory, suggesting that antebellum slave-traders transported black leopards from Africa, then lost or released them into the wilds of Dixie. Authors Loren Coleman and Mark Hall propose a more startling solution—namely, survival into modern times of the prehistoric cave lion *Panthera leo atrox*. Coleman and Hall surmise that sexual dimorphism produced black females of the species, while the males resembled oversized African lions. I'm not convinced of this. Although flatly rejected by mainstream science, the notion serves double duty, explaining various reports since 1939 wherein black and tawny cats (the latter often sporting bushy manes) were seen together, roaming from New Brunswick and Connecticut to Indiana and Ohio.[35]

A Bluegrass Tiger

Kentucky's earliest recorded ABC encounter is both unique and regrettably vague. It appeared in Boston's *New England Farmer* on August 3, 1823, as a dispatch from Russellville (Logan County), describing "a tiger of a brindle color with a most terrific front—his eyes are described as the largest ever seen in any animal."[36] Four witnesses observed the cat, including two armed with rifles who:

> ...fired on him at the distance of 50 yards without forcing him to move from his stand; a furious look and appalling brow frightened the two men without guns who fled to town. Experienced marksmen continued to fire, and on the 12th shot the beast put off at full speed....
>
> ...When the news reached Russellville about 40 gentlemen repaired to the spot, and had a full view of the ground. The print which the paws of the animal made in the earth corresponds with the account given of his great bulk by those who had an opportunity of viewing him at a short distance for several minutes....
>
> ...The above tiger was seen a few days after braving a dozen shots and making its way into the state of Tennessee, and there is still a prospect of its being taken.[37]

There the story ends, suggesting that riflemen in the Volunteer State were no more skilled than those in Russellville. Bart Nunnelly's description of the unknown cat as "striped," with "eyes the size of dinner plates" seems to embroider the original report. Likewise, his suggestion that the "phantom tiger" was "spectral in nature and could not be killed" probably credits the frightened marksmen with too much composure.[38]

10.
Tigers, while native to Asia, sometimes appear in Kentucky.
Image Courtesy of U.S. Fish & Wildlife Service

Exotics and Unknowns

Two final ABC reports come from the town of California, in Kentucky's Campbell County, and from Pine Hill in Rockcastle County. Loren Coleman reports the first case, from 1977, and while he distinguishes the cat from "panthers" seen in other states that year, no other details are provided. Research involving Campbell County's library proved fruitless. Coleman does, however, promise further details for future study. Bart Nunnelly credits the Pine Hill sighting to several unnamed witnesses who saw a creature "bigger than a cat but smaller than a cougar." It climbed trees and had a "row of spikes" along its back that may have been an optical illusion or a ridge or ruffled fur.[39]

11.
Servals, sometimes kept as pets, are sometimes found in the wild. *Image Courtesy of U.S. Fish & Wildlife Service*

Exotic feline species do exist within Kentucky, although no great cats have yet been killed or captured. Barbara Rosenman, in Oldham County, has collected road-killed exotics including an African serval (*Leptailurus serval*) and an Asian reed cat (*Felis chaus*), also called a jungle cat or swamp lynx. Both are sold as pets in the United States, by establishments such as Valley Stables and Exotic Livestock in Berea, Kentucky.[40]

3.
Cold-Blooded Creatures

Kentucky wildlife authorities recognize fifty-one species of native reptiles, including thirteen turtles, eight lizards, and thirty snakes.[1] Those known as natives of the Bluegrass State do not concern us here, as we pursue exotic species and assorted giants that do not resemble any species known on Earth.

Alligators Astray

Herpetologists tell us that American alligators (*Alligator mississippiensis*) are alien to Kentucky. Their normal range extends from the Carolinas southward through Florida, and eastward across Georgia, Alabama, Mississippi, Louisiana, southern Arkansas, and eastern Texas. It is conceivable that they might navigate the Mississippi River to wash ashore in far-southwestern Kentucky, but no current sources acknowledge any crocodilian population in the state.[2]

That fact, however, has not kept the large aquatic reptiles from appearing in Kentucky, any more than it has barred them from the lakes, rivers, and storm drains of New York, Los Angeles, Detroit, Toronto, or a host of other sites hundreds of miles beyond their normal range.[3]

In every case, regardless of the alligator's size, officials blame the incidents on unnamed private owners who presumably release their pets deliberately or lose them through sheer negligence. The miscreants in question never voluntarily surrender, nor have any within living memory been traced via detective work. Still, the explanation seems a fair one, given the flourishing trade in reptiles—and anything seems preferable to contending with a breeding population of home-grown gators.

Jim Harrison, founder of the Kentucky Reptile Zoo in Slade, Kentucky (Powell County), observed in May 2004 that "you can buy anything on the Internet except common sense." Despite a state law banning private possession of crocodilians, alligators still find homes where they do not belong and cannot be controlled with any certainty. In 2000 alone, Harrison reportedly collected fourteen alligators in Kentucky, Indiana, and Ohio.[4] Closing the door on imports, however, seems to be an insoluble problem.

A case in point was reported from Oak Grove (Christian County) in September 2005. There, a 54-inch gator escaped from the rear of a moving pickup truck and fled into the basement of a nearby home. Residents caught it and drove it to a pet store in nearby Clarksville, Tennessee, but the story did not end there. According to the *Clarksville Leaf-Chronicle*, "it was being brought back to Kentucky when it escaped again." DFWR officers called off their search on September 7, comparing it to the proverbial hunt for a needle in a haystack, but private parties captured the scaly fugitive one day later. This time, officials said it would be taken to an unnamed "nearby zoo."[5]

An alarming alligator story circulated via emails during early April 2008, reporting that a huge alligator had been found at Lake Cumberland, a man-made lake that sprawls over 104 square miles in the counties of Clinton, Laurel, McCreary, Pulaski, Russell, and Wayne. Reporters from KTBS-TV allegedly spotted the gator while circling the lake in their station's helicopter, after which game warden Joe Goff arrived to kill the record-breaking twenty-three-footer in a residential yard at Monticello. A photo of the gator, hoisted aloft with Goff in the background, accompanied the message as a testament to its veracity. Journalists swallowed the bait...and soon learned that the tale was a hoax.[6]

12.
This hoaxed Internet photo depicts the alleged capture of an alligator at Lake Cumberland in 2008.
Image Courtesy of Author's Collection

For starters, KTBS-TV is based in Shreveport, Louisiana, and it has no helicopter (as of this printing). Neither did Kentucky's Department of Fish and Wildlife Resources employ anyone named "Joe Goff." The photo was legitimate, but only to a point. Its subject was an alligator of normal size, killed somewhere in Louisiana (with Spanish moss visible in the background) and photographed by members of the U.S. Army Corps of Engineers. Photoshop technology was then employed to couple the reptile with an unknown khaki-clad officer—whose shadow somehow crept beneath the gator's tail as he walked past it.[7]

Hoaxes aside, one author who disputes the official view of how alligators land far outside their normal range is Loren Coleman. In his book, *Mysterious America*, he suggests that certain crocodilians "teleport" themselves through space, thereby explaining cases wherein they appear to drop from the sky. Thus far, no mainstream scientist has endorsed Coleman's theory.[8]

Leaping Lizards

The largest of Kentucky's eight known native lizards is the legless slender glass lizard (*Ophisaurus attenuatus*), with a record length of 42 inches. The largest species of conventional appearance is the 9.5-inch 6-lined racerunner (*Cnemidophorus sexlineatus sexlineatus*), followed by the 8.5-inch 5-lined skink (*Eumeces fasciatus*). No known species in the state—or any native to the U.S.A.—approaches the dimensions of the Old World monitors (*family Varanidae*), whose number includes the 10-foot Komodo dragon.[9]

13. No known living lizard is larger than the Komodo dragon. *Image Courtesy of U.S. National Oceanic and Atmospheric Administration*

Nonetheless, a much larger lizard appeared in Trimble County during July 1975. Milton resident Carl Abbott filed the first report of nocturnal "grunts and groans" in a field near his house, where he photographed a five-inch footprint with "deeply embedded claws." Soon afterward, Clarence Cabell saw a "huge" lizard prowling a junkyard behind his Blue Grass Body Shop. Cabell said the reptile had "big eyes similar to frog's....Beneath its mouth was an off-white color, and there were black and white stripes cross ways of its body, with quarter-size orange speckles over it." Cable's brother Garrett saw the lizard on July 27, but it was gone when he returned with Clarence. On July 28, Garrett saw another reptile, larger than the first one at an estimated fifteen feet. It fled after he lobbed a stone at it, then ran to fetch a rifle, and apparently the beast has not returned.[10]

That relatively simple story has been altered and expanded over time. Authors Loren Coleman and Jerome Clark placed the Cabell sightings in October, while researcher Mark Hall claimed that the lizard ran bipedally, on its hind legs. From there, Internet author Albert Rosales described the beast as "a giant lizard man type humanoid," presumably descended from a UFO.[11]

Clarence Cabell offered a more mundane solution to the mystery, suggesting that one or more monitor lizards might have hatched from eggs laid in the junkyard. Monitors are Old World lizards, but many are kept as exotic pets throughout the United States and some—including the Nile monitor (*Varanus niloticus*) and the Australian lace monitor (*V. varius*)—display patterns of spots and stripes resembling those of the Milton "monster." Neither of those officially reach fifteen feet, but Earth's largest lizard—the Komodo dragon (*V. komodoensis*)—may exceed ten feet in length. The monitor solution clearly seems more reasonable than the suggestion of a huge unknown amphibian, which would in any case suffer from dehydration without water, in a junkyard's summer heat.[12]

Hall theoretically links the Milton sightings to an earlier event reported from Warren County, Ohio, vaguely dating from "the late 1800s." There, near Crosswick, two boys were fishing in the Little Miami River when one was attacked by a giant lizard, which dragged him toward a pit beneath a massive sycamore tree. Three nearby workmen heard the child's screams and found him grappling with "a reptilian creature, thirty to forty feet long and about sixteen inches in diameter with scaled legs and body; the head, which was the same thickness as the body, was split by a large mouth with fangs and a forked tongue." The lizard dropped its prey as they approached, and later escaped, running swiftly on its hind legs, when a party of sixty armed men returned to cut down the tree. Author Chris Woodyard claims that the reptile was later seen at Shaker's Swamp, near Lebanon and Caesar Creek, but once again eluded hunters. No living lizard known to science matches the description of the Crosswick monster.[13]

Yet another apparent bipedal reptile surfaced in central Kentucky on February 11, 2009. A trucker known only as "Marvin" was southbound on I-75, somewhere between Richmond (Madison County) and Williamsburg (Whitley County), when he logged the strange encounter at 2:15 a.m. Suddenly, a gray, hairless, rabbit-sized creature resembling "a small dinosaur" ran across the highway, twenty feet in front of Marvin's truck. Despite his surprise and the animal's speed, Marvin noted the creature's long tail and "small dark eye on the side of its head." As he described the thing, in a report logged on the Kentucky Bigfoot website, "It truly looked like something out of Jurassic Park."[14]

Snakes in the Grass

Kentucky's DFWR recognizes thirty snake species as natives of the Bluegrass State. Kentucky's largest is the eastern coachwhip (*Masticophis flagellum flagellum*), with a record length of eight-feet-six inches, followed closely by the black rat snake (*Elaphe obsoleta obsoleta*) at eight-feet-five inches. The state's largest venomous snake is the timber rattler (*Crotalus horridus*), with a record length of six-feet-two inches.[15]

14.
The eastern coachwhip is Kentucky's largest known snake. *Image Courtesy of U.S. Fish & Wildlife Service*

Kentucky paranormal researcher Jan Thompson reports aboriginal traditions of a giant aquatic serpent known as losa sinti, dwelling in Bluegrass swamps and rivers, where it fed on deer, coyotes, and occasional careless children. Friendly tribesmen warned white settlers of the danger from such reptiles in the early 1800s, but no specific reports of sightings have yet been uncovered.[16]

Eyewitness accounts of giant snakes at large in Kentucky date from August 24, 1830, when Norwalk, Ohio's Huron Reflector announced that a "snake of extraordinary dimensions...18 or 20 feet in length, and as thick as an ordinary stove pipe," had been seen near Lexington. Hunters had "traced him to his cave" but failed to bag the serpent, despite the lure of a $500 reward for its capture.[17]

The next account, from September 1857, comes to us in garbled, roundabout fashion from Harlan County. The source is an unnamed Virginia resident, described in print as "a gentleman in whom implicit confidence may be placed," speaking to the Abington (Indiana) *Democrat* and quoted in the *Weyauwegian* of Weyauwega, Wisconsin. The anonymous informant claimed that residents of "Harlem County," while picking berries "about three weeks ago," had roused an "enormous" foul-smelling serpent by dropping stones into a cave. Armed men rallied and killed the beast, which proved to be a twenty-foot rattlesnake "with 28 rattles—the first was four inches in diameter, the rest decreasing in size to the last." The snake's skin was reportedly placed on display, but no trace of it now remains. We should note here that the largest known rattlesnake, the eastern diamondback (*Crotalus adamanteus*), does not officially exceed eight feet in length.[18]

15.
No venomous snake known in Kentucky grows larger than the timber rattler. *Image Courtesy of U.S. Fish & Wildlife Service*

In June 1880, the *Waterloo Courier* (Iowa) reported an 18-foot snake haunting Spencer County. According to that report, "There is a tradition that such a reptile escaped from a circus in that county many years since and that it still lives."[19]

Another huge rattlesnake surfaced at Rocky Hill in June 1883, but the *Defiance Democrat's* (Ohio) report does not distinguish between Rocky Hill in Barren County or another town of the same name in Edmonson County. In either case, Dr. J.B. Thomas was cutting wheat on his farm with several employees when they met and killed a rattler nine-foot-seven inches long, and fourteen inches in circumference. Dr. Thomas extracted the snake's 1.5-inch fangs as souvenirs, then shipped its carcass off for exhibition at druggist L.M. Ewing's shop. Ewing, in turn, photographed the snake and sent its picture to another pharmacist in Smith's Grove (Warren County). As usual in such cases, neither the photo nor any part of the reptile exists today.[20]

Noble Bean, of Crittenden County, claimed sightings of an even larger rattlesnake near Heath Mountain in February 1917. He planned to catch the snake alive and sell it to a circus for $1,000 but was not successful. Still, as reported in the *New York Times*, he "got close enough to the ugly reptile to estimate its dimensions, which are about the circumference of the average telephone post and length of some twelve feet, with rattlers about a foot long."[21]

Elisha Highlander, a farmhand at Bee Lick (Pulaski County), killed a "cow snake" more than nine feet long on G.E. Linville's farm, after "a spirited combat" in September 1918. "Cow snake" is a local name for the black rat snake, whose record length of eight-foot-four inches falls below the size claimed by Bean—though not by much.[22]

Henry Ross and his wife were returning to their home in Paris (Bourbon County) during early February 1921, when they saw an apparent black-and-white auto tire lying in the middle of the highway. Ross stopped his car and went to claim the "tire," then hastily retreated as it uncoiled and crawled into the roadside weeds. According to the *Orlean Evening Herald* (New York), the snake was "a boa constrictor, the property of a carnival company that met disaster in a cloudburst" near Paris on some unspecified date. Carnival workers later recaptured the snake—which, from Ross's description, did not resemble a boa constrictor but may have been a python.[23]

Four decades passed before the next large snake appeared, in Calloway County, in June 1962. Farmer Hildred Paschall of Hazel was first to meet the reptile, on June 6 or 12 (reports differ), describing it as twenty-four to thirty feet long and "as big around as a stove pipe." Ernie Collins, a carnival snake-handler, investigated Paschall's sighting on June 20 and reported his findings to Dr. Hunter Hancock, a biology professor at nearby Murray State University. Aside from belly tracks, Collins found squirrel nests raided by the reptile twenty feet above the forest floor. Based on its size and Paschall's rough description of the serpent's markings, Collins guessed that it might be an Indian python (*Python molurus*).[24]

16.
Thousands of pythons are kept as pets in the United States. *Image Courtesy of U.S. National Oceanic and Atmospheric Administration*

Those reports brought armed snake-hunters out in droves around Hazel, prompting Sheriff Woodrow Rickman to complain, "It would be less dangerous to approach the snake with a switch than to face the wild drivers on the highway and the indiscriminate use of firearms near the scene." Excitement escalated on June 29, when a motorist named Bivens saw the snake crossing Highway 893 near Crossland (misspelled "Grassland" in newspaper reports). When Bivens saw the snake, its body stretched across the twenty-foot-wide highway with its head and tail concealed by weeds on either side. Based on the latest description, an unnamed biology teacher from Benton (Marshall County) speculated that the snake might be an anaconda (*Eunectes murinus*). The *Greenville*

Democrat Times (Mississippi) claimed that "[r]esidents of the area, who say there have been reports of a monster snake for the past fifteen years, were hopeful that someday it would become as famous as the Loch Ness monster."[25]

Our next report appeared in *Fate* magazine's December 1965 issue, penned by late publisher Curtis Fuller. It read: "Then there are reports of a giant snake inhabiting seventy-acre Reynolds Lake near LaGrange in Oldham County, Kentucky. Several persons said they saw the creature, its body as big around as a stovepipe and a head with large, beady eyes. Supposedly it had eaten all the fish and frogs in the lake and was now seriously considering the hogs. One thing was sure, the hogs were now being quartered elsewhere as a precaution." Fuller listed no sources for his report, and while no map or other published source at my disposal provides directions to a Reynolds Lake in Kentucky, Graham Troop at the Oldham County Library says that "the rough consensus seems to be that Reynolds Lake is near Ballardsville, on or near Mt. Zion Road." There the matter rests, with no further reports of large snakes in the area.[26]

We next leap forward to the 1980s, when Bart Nunnelly's uncle James regaled him with an undated personal encounter from Stanley, in Daviess County. James Nunnelly was picnicking with his wife at a rural pond, when they saw a huge snake crawling over nearby logs. Retreating to their car, they watched the snake for several minutes but "never did see either end of it." James described the reptile as muddy-brown in color, with "some kind of pattern on its back resembling a rattler's." Around the same time, two men in Henderson County saw a large snake crawl into a hole "beneath the Fifth Street overpass across from the old saw mill." While uncertain of its length, they compared its diameter to a six-inch pipe.[27]

Future reports of large exotic snakes will likely be explained with reference to the global trade in boas and pythons, sold through various pet shops and Internet websites throughout the United States. Burmese pythons released by negligent owners have established breeding colonies in Florida, and the two-foot-long python found in a rental car at Paducah, Kentucky, in May 2006 was almost certainly a fugitive.[28]

As for the others who have frightened Bluegrass residents since 1830—long before the traffic in exotics was established—and the giant rattlers still unknown to science, we can only speculate. For now, the quest must end as it began, in mystery.

4.
Freshwater Phantoms

Worldwide, some 900 lakes and rivers lay claim to large unidentified creatures. Scotland's Loch Ness is the most famous, with "Nessie" sightings spanning 1,400 years, but worthy North American rivals include Lake Champlain (with "Champ"), Lake Tahoe ("Tessie"), and British Columbia's Okanagan Lake ("Ogopogo").[1]

Kentucky's tally of freshwater phantoms is average, including four unknown creatures and several others seriously out of place. Unlike most U.S. states, however, which boast aboriginal legends of aquatic monsters dating from prehistory, recorded sightings from the Bluegrass State begin in the latter years of the Twentieth Century.

Herrington Lake

17.
Herrington Lake. *Image Courtesy of U.S. Fish & Wildlife Service*

This Mercer County reservoir, located thirty miles south of Lexington, was created in 1924, when engineers employed by the Kentucky Power Company dammed the Dix River. Forty-four years passed before Lawrence Thomas, a professor of classics at the University of Kentucky, bought a home at Herrington Lake and determined that there was "something out there." Another four years slipped away before Thomas told his story to the press, in August 1972.[2]

According to Thomas, a "monster" inhabits Herrington Lake, taking leisurely swims between Chenault Bridge and Wells Landing in the early-morning hours. After four years of sporadic observation, he had only seen its piglike snout and curly tail above the surface, separated by a gap of fifteen feet while the beast swam "at about the speed of a boat with a trolling motor." The animal was strange but inoffensive, prompting Thomas to explain that "it's a monster only in the sense that you'd call an alligator or a crocodile a monster if nobody else had ever seen one."[3]

With so little evidence to work from, Thomas surmised that his beast might have evaded human observation "since its ancestors swam up the Mississippi and Ohio rivers millennia ago." While unable to guess its identity, the professor suggested that "many generations of monsters could have survived in a cave submerged when the dam was built, to venture forth when the new avenue became available."[4]

Perhaps, but as of press time for this book, no other witnesses have gone on record with reports of unknown creatures paddling around Herrington Lake.

A Giant Turtle

Our next report comes from Brad Nunnelly, whose record for personal sightings of unknown creatures seems to be unrivaled in Kentucky's history. The incident occurred sometime in 1983, when Nunnelly and two of his brothers were fishing along the Ohio River, near downtown Henderson. They spied an object the size of a Volkswagen Beetle floating downstream, some thirty feet out from the shore. It was light tan in color, partially covered with moss, while its bare spots revealed a pattern resembling the scutes (scales) on the carapace of a turtle's shell. Moments later, Nunnelly determined that it was a turtle, when the creature "poked its head out from beneath the shell and looked around."[5]

Bart acknowledges that no VW-sized turtles are known to dwell in the Ohio River. In fact, no living turtle of such size is recognized on Earth today. The largest known turtle—the leatherback (*Dermochelys coriacea*)— is a marine species with a record length of eight feet, while the largest terrestrial tortoises (from the Galápagos Islands) boast shells three feet five inches long. Meanwhile, North America's largest freshwater turtle is the alligator snapper (*Macroclemys temminicki*), with a record length of 31.5 inches. Its official range in far-western Kentucky does not include Henderson County, and while a stray specimen might swim farther eastward along the Ohio, none approach the size of Nunnelly's giant.[6]

18.
America's largest freshwater turtle, the alligator snapper. *Image Courtesy of U.S. Fish & Wildlife Service*

To find a turtle of that size, we must go back in time to the Cretaceous Period, when a massive marine species known today as Archelon plied the seas covering modern North America. From fossil remains, chiefly concentrated in Kansas, Nebraska, and South Dakota, we know that Archelon exceeded 13 feet in length and tipped the scales around 4,500 pounds. Paleontologists insist that the species has been extinct for some 70 million years, and that it never shared the planet with our proto-human ancestors.[7]

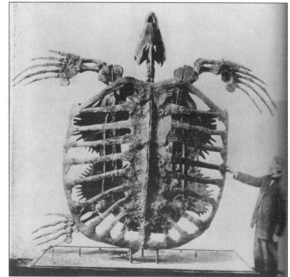

19.
Fossil remains of the prehistoric turtle Archelon. *Image Courtesy of Author's Collection*

"Genny"

While Nunnelly's giant turtle passed through Henderson County enroute to parts unknown, a larger unknown beast took its place and appeared to set up housekeeping. The first encounter with the creature nicknamed "Genny"—for Geneva, west of Henderson on the Ohio River—occurred on some unspecified date in the late 1980s. Two young hunters, identified only as "Andy A." and "Mike B.," were sniping at turtles in the 10,600-acre Sloughs Wildlife Management Area, while Mike's father waited in a car parked nearby. After shooting several hapless reptiles, the boys saw "something" surface in the river.[8]

The object first appeared as a green "hump," resembling a moss-covered automobile tire, but with darker green circles the size of baseballs regularly spaced along its side facing the boys. As Mike and Andy watched, more humps appeared, totaling five in all. The boys surmised that they were looking at a chain of tires, connected in some way—until a large reptilian head appeared, scanning the river's bank with black eyes set above an elongated snout. Upon seeing the boys, the thirty-foot creature submerged and did not rise again.[9]

Bart Nunnelly interviewed "Andy A." in 1998 and again in 2005. Together, they produced a sketch of Genny that resembles nothing known to science, an apparent snake whose vertical undulations defy the capability of a reptilian spine.[10]

A midget version of Genny appeared to witness James Kennedy, two miles from the scene of the 1980s incident, on July 4, 2001. Kennedy described the creature as three feet long and serpentine, with "a beak which resembled a duck's." Unlike a normal water snake, it swam with its head raised above the surface and revealed no fear of Kennedy, cavorting in shallow water near shore for two hours. Kennedy later told Bart Nunnelly that he could have captured it easily, but had left his fishing net at home.[11]

Green River

20.
Kentucky's Green River.
*Image Courtesy of U.S.
Fish & Wildlife Service*

Kentucky's Green River is a tributary of the Ohio, rising in Lincoln County and flowing westward for 300 miles. Bart Nunnelly describes it as "one of the deepest rivers in the world, second only to South America's Amazon," but official websites dispute that claim, reporting an average depth of ten feet. Nonetheless, the Green River has produced several of Kentucky's record gamefish, including a ninety-seven-pound flathead catfish, a fifty-two-pound bighead carp, and a thirty-eight-pound freshwater drum.[10]

And it also produced our next aquatic monster sighting.

The witness, once again, was Bart Nunnelly, crossing the Spottsville Bridge at Beals, enroute to his job in Owensboro, on some unspecified morning in 1998. Noting a disturbance in the water below, Nunnelly focused on "two slender objects, each about fifteen to twenty feet long, apparently engaged in the act of fighting each other." Deprived of a clear view by pre-dawn darkness, Nunnelly assumed that the creatures were giant catfish rumored to inhabit the Green River, but later revised that opinion based on their slender physiques.[11]

After his personal experience, Nunnelly recorded a fisherman's tale from the early 1980s, describing a vaguely similar creature seen in the same general area. The unnamed angler reported a long, slender beast "of immense proportions" crawling ashore near the spot where Nunnelly logged his sighting. Atop its head, two horns or antennae resembling a snail's eye-stalks were clearly visible. As the unknown animal crept toward him, the fisherman hastily fled.[12]

Freshwater Cephalopods

Cephalopods (from the Greek, "head-foot") are mollusks characterized by prominent heads from which multiple arms or tentacles protrude. Science presently recognizes 786 living species, including the squids, octopuses, nautiloids, and cuttlefish. They inhabit every sea and ocean of the world, from pole to pole. Without exception, all are said to be marine species, yet multiple reports describe freshwater specimens, including four accounts from Kentucky.[13]

Our first two reports come from Campbell County, during early 1959. On January 30, a creature described as "gray, with a lopsided chest, 'ugly' tentacles, and rolls of fat surrounding a 'bald head'" crawled ashore from the Licking River, near Covington. It was not photographed or captured, but a witnesses reported a similar beast bobbing in the Ohio River, near Fort Thomas, a few days later.[14]

Another four decades elapsed before an octopus was found on the Indiana side of the Ohio River, at Falls of the Ohio State Park, on November 21, 1999. Tourists discovered the animal beached on the park's fossil bed and alerted employee Paul McLean, who photographed it and reported that "it was not alive and it was not in a state of decomposition. It probably weighed less than a pound and the color shown in the picture is close to accurate." Dominic Foster, curator of the park's aquarium, created an exhibit for the octopus, but strangely discarded the carcass itself.[15]

21.
An octopus found beside the Ohio River in 1999. *Image Courtesy of Paul McClean*

While Foster identified the specimen as an Atlantic octopus (*Octopus vulgaris*), John Forsythe, a researcher at the National Resource Center for Cephalopods at the University of Texas Medical Branch in Galveston, reviewed McLean's photo and announced that it was either a Caribbean armstripe octopus (*O. burryi*) or a bumblebee two-stripe octopus (*O. filosus*), also found in the Caribbean and Gulf of Mexico.[16]

In any case, how did an ocean-dwelling specimen from the Eastern Seaboard or the Caribbean find its way to the Ohio River? The best official guess involves a pet discarded by its owner, but the mystery remains unsolved.[17]

On August 7, 2006, David Stepp of Jeffersonville, Indiana, was fishing along the Ohio River when he hooked an octopus with a six-foot arm span, tip to tip. He tossed the animal into the trunk of his car and drove to Clarksville, where he showed his catch to a policeman and Bill Putt, a ranger at Falls of the Ohio State Park. Once again, Paul McLean was summoned to photograph the creature, but this time the mystery was quickly solved. One day after the story aired, on August 10, Louisville college student Zachary Treitz accepted blame for the incident. Treitz told the *Courier-Journal* that he had purchased the dead octopus from a local seafood shop and videotaped it in the river as part of a class film project. "I guess we didn't think about the interest this would cause," he said. "It was completely surprising."[18]

Was a similar prank responsible for the carcass found in 1999? And what of the living cephalopods reported from Campbell County forty years earlier? Researchers Chad Arment and Brad LaGrange conclude that the existence of freshwater cephalopods "does not appear to be biologically impossible; merely biologically improbable."[19] For mainstream scientists, the case is far from proved.

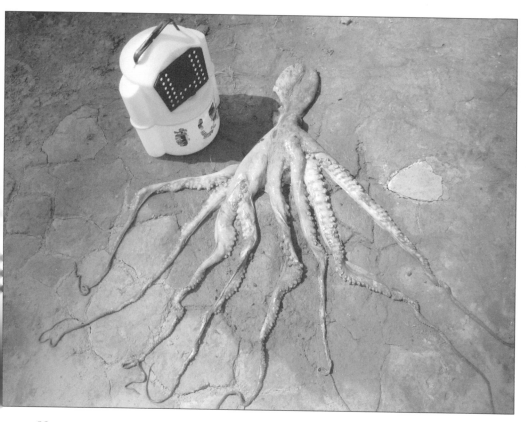

22.
Another octopus, found near the same location in 2006.
Image Courtesy of Paul McClean

5.

Big Feet

Throughout North America, witnesses report sightings of large bipedal primates presently unknown to science. Personal encounters number in the thousands since the early Nineteenth Century, while discoveries of large humanoid footprints in unlikely places far outnumber sightings of the animals themselves. Mainstream zoologists insist that all sightings of the creatures commonly called Bigfoot or Sasquatch result from hoaxes or misidentification of known species such as bears, deer, and so forth. Still, the sightings continue in ever-increasing numbers.[1]

While the Pacific Northwest produces the majority of Bigfoot sightings, every U.S. state except Hawaii has cases on file. Kentucky boasts more than its share of reported encounters. No two sources agree on the total number of Bluegrass reports, but my survey of published works and Internet websites reveals 225 specific cases logged between the late Eighteenth Century and November 2008. Nine other accounts refer vaguely to "multiple," "many," or "ongoing" incidents reported between the World War II and the 1990s.[2]

From Prehistory to Independence

As in other states from coast to coast, Kentucky's aboriginal tribes left evidence of "beast-men" in their prehistoric artwork. Researcher and self-proclaimed Bigfoot witness Bart Nunnelly cites evidence from three locations, including the Asphalt Rock pictograph site (in Edmonson County, southwest of New Liberty Church), Powell County's Ledford Hollow pictograph site, and "Carter Caves National Park" (actually Carter Caves State Resort Park, along Tygarts Creek in Carter County).[3]

23.
A portrait of
Bigfoot, based on
eyewitness de-
scriptions. *Artwork
Courtesy of William
Rebsamen*

   According to Nunnelly, the Asphalt Rock site includes a rock painting
of "a bizarre humanoid figure" portrayed with "a cat-like, apparently
muzzled face, hairy body and either horns or pointed ears." Prehistoric
art at Ledford Hollow—where a modern Bigfoot sighting was reported
in November 2006—include carvings of four-toed humanoid footprints
resembling aberrant primate tracks reported from various parts of North
America (and the world at large) over the past century. Nunnelly cites no
specific hominid art forms from Carter Caves, but claims "at least 12"
undated Bigfoot sightings from that vicinity. Finally, he says that "other
petroglyphic sites exist throughout the state which contain images which
depict similar 4, 5, and even 6-toed non human looking footprints."[4]

24.
Carter Caves,
alleged scene of
multiple Bigfoot
sightings. *Image
Courtesy of U.S. Fish
& Wildlife Service*

Our first account of a primate encounter with white settlers comes from frontiersman Daniel Boone, although its import is disputed even among Bigfoot believers. According to historian and Boone biographer John Faragher, Boone once regaled dinner companions with his account of killing a ten-foot hairy giant which he called a "Yahoo." No date is offered either for the conversation or the incident itself, but Faragher suggests that Boone borrowed the name from a race of giants described in the novel *Gulliver's Travels* (1726). Finally, Faragher dismisses the story as "a tall tale that Boone repeated to a number of people during his last year [1820], one such as he would have told in a winter camp." Despite that judgment, some Bigfoot researchers still regard Boone's story as a true account.[4]

25.
Frontiersman Daniel Boone
claimed to have killed a hairy
"Yahoo" in Kentucky. *Image
Courtesy of Author's Collection*

The Nineteenth Century

Daniel Boone was dead for half a century before Kentucky logged its next report of unknown primates, from Allen County. Details are vague, but Canadian researcher John Green, writing in 1978, refers to 100-year-old stories of creatures inhabiting a valley called "Monkey Cave Hollow."[5] Sometime in the 1960s, Harold Holland of Scottsville wrote to late author Ivan Sanderson, reporting that:

> About 20 years ago one old man who had moved from this area but returned for a final visit to his home, told me that when he was a boy of about 7 or 8 years, he saw the carcass of the last "monkey." He stated that a hunter came by his father's house and displayed the dead beast. He said that he could not recall exactly what it looked like (after all it had been 80 years or thereabouts) but that the creature had hands and feet "like a person" and was about the same size as himself, had no tail and was covered with brown hair.[6]

Kentucky's next "wild man" was a Tennessee import, transported to Louisville by Dr. G.C. Broyler for display by "manager Whallen of the Metropolitan," described in print as a one-third owner of the "mysterious and wonderful creature."[7] According to the *Courier-Journal's* report of October 24, 1878:

> At a distance the general outline of his figure would indicate that he is only an ordinary man. Close inspection shows that his whole body is covered with a layer of scales, which drop off at regular intervals, in the spring and fall, like the skin of a rattlesnake. He has a heavy growth of hair on his head and a dark reddish beard about six inches long. His eyes present a frightful appearance, being at least twice the size of the average-sized eye. Some of his toes are formed together, which give his feet a strange appearance, and his height, when standing perfectly erect, is about six-foot-five inches.... His entire body must be wet at intervals, and, should this be neglected, he begins immediately to manifest great uneasiness, his flesh becomes feverish, and his suffering cannot be alleviated until the water is applied.[8]

Although habitually included in collections of early Bigfoot reports, the creature described here bears little resemblance to a "normal" Sasquatch. Its scales suggest one of the "lizard men" described in Chapter 6, although the molting process must be fabricated, since the subject had not been observed to shed his skin. The captive may have been a man afflicted with some skin disease or combination of deformities—and, then again, the story may have been a total fabrication, since no further record of the "wild man" presently exists.

A more conventional "wild man" appeared to residents of Lewis County during summer 1892. Dr. H.W. Dimmit of Vanceburg described it to the *Ohio Democrat* "as being of gigantic stature, covered with a thick growth of hair and is fierce and untamable." One witness tried to converse with the creature, whereupon it pelted him with stones until he fled.[9]

Two years later, in 1894, residents of Deep Creek (Mercer County) blamed an albino "man-beast" for stealing their chickens, eggs, piglets, lambs, and other edibles. Farmer Eph Boston and his sons observed the prowler when it stole three chickens from their barn, describing it as six-foot-six inches tall, with "cat-like" hands and clawed feet. Gunshots drove it off, apparently without inflicting any injury, but the creature did not go far. Witness Joseph Ewalt subsequently saw it, describing the creature's "great long white hair hanging down from his head and face that was as coarse as a horse's mane. His legs were covered with hair and the only article of clothing he wore was a piece of sheepskin over the lower portion of his body, reaching nearly for his knees." Ewalt also claimed that "a light came from his eyes and mouth similar to fire." Curiously, while the *Courier-Journal* reported those events in May 1894, with an article reprinted in the *Daily Courant* from Hartford, Connecticut, the *Evening News* of Lincoln, Nebraska, ran the same story on November 14, dating Eph Boston's sighting from "early Sunday" (i.e., November 11, 1894).[10]

Early Twentieth Century

Reno, Nevada's *Evening Gazette* reported the next Kentucky "wild man" sighting on March 27, 1907. According to that story, farmhand Jim Peters was working in the woods near Buena Vista (Garrard County) when his dog began barking and "showing every evidence of extreme fright." Peters then observed a manlike creature whose "long black hair streamed down its back and breast in a matted mass, and covered the face so that he could not see whether it had a beard of not. Its body was covered with a coat of soft, fuzzy black hair and its finger and toe nails were long and curved like talons." Oddly, the figure also wore a raccoon skin "tied around its loins."[11]

Garrard County adjoins Mercer, to the southeast, and while a loincloth-wearing hermit would not require thirteen years to cover that distance on foot, it seems unlikely that his hair would change from white to black with age.

Our next report, never previously published, comes from witness Jewell Castle, a Kentucky native now residing in Indiana. One night in the 1930s, after dining with relatives at Haldeman (Rowan County), Castle's family was startled by "a loud and terrible noise" at the kitchen door. Seconds later, an apelike creature tried to force its way inside the house. As Castle recalls the event:

It tried to push the door open with its body, but all the men pushed the table against the door and pushed back with all their might. It had a terrible odor about it. It almost got the door pushed in, but they managed to hang in there and it went away. They grabbed their guns and went out to see what it was. It had giant foot prints—none that they could identify. They couldn't locate it that night, but next morning they followed the tracks as best they could, then lost them. We were used to hearing sounds of panthers and other wild animals, but this animal sounded much bigger and louder than any they ever heard and it scared all of us. They called it "Big Foot" due to the size of the foot prints they had followed. We never heard it again, thank goodness.[12]

Most authors credit coinage of the "Bigfoot" name to California journalists or road construction workers, following a spate of incidents around Bluff Creek in 1958, expanding from there to the point where unknown primates wear that tag from North America to Southeast Asia and Australia. Castle's story represents the first known usage of the label, though it was not widely known.[13]

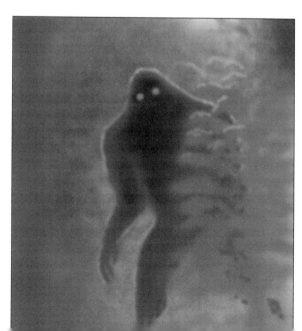

26.
The "Bigfoot" term was coined by Kentucky residents in the 1930s. *Artwork Courtesy of William Rebsamen*

Another decade passed before the next Kentucky Bigfoot sighting was reported, albeit reluctantly, in April 1944. Nurse Shirley Elkins was working the night shift at a hospital in Paintsville (Johnson County), when a local fisherman arrived with his mother, seeking emergency treatment. The man was "all a mess of scratches," acting nervous, but he followed his mother's instruction to "just say he fell down." Doctors kept him overnight for observation, and received a phone call later in the evening concerning a car crash caused by "a tall hairy creature" crossing the highway. Time passed, and Elkins left nursing to work at a restaurant owned by her former patient. They married in June 1945, whereupon he finally told her the truth about his former injuries.[14]

According to that story, Ellis Elkins was cleaning catfish behind the riverside café at dusk, when a shaggy, snarling biped approached, shoved him, and grabbed for the fish. Ellis fought back with an empty bottle, at first believing his assailant was a teenager dressed in an ape suit. A close-up view of its fangs and "aqua-color eyes, like a cat" changed his mind. Aside from that, the six-foot creature had large feet with nails like claws, a coat of shiny slate-gray hair, and a tail that "bushed" when it saw the catfish. Ellis and his mother withheld the story from fear that anyone he told would think him "nuts or drunk."[15]

Likewise, a Perry County report from the late 1940s went unpublished until June 1997, when researcher Brad LaGrange relayed it to the International Bigfoot Society. Trappers Ed Laven, Res Shoemaker, and Jerry LaGrange (Brad's father) recalled hearing strange cries at night, "like a female screaming," which they later concluded was Bigfoot. Similar cries had been heard since the 1920s, attributed by skeptics to bobcats or screech owls.[16]

Our last report—or, rather, series of reports—from the first half of the Twentieth Century is shrouded in confusion and may not involve Bigfoot at all, though it appears in limited detail on the Gulf Coast Bigfoot Research Organization's website. Other sources describe the beast in questions as a "goatman," which is covered fully in Chapter 6. For the record, though, we must consider the elusive creature known to residents of Jefferson County as the Pope Lick Monster.

Pope Lick Creek lies fifteen miles east of Louisville, spanned by a Norfolk Southern Railway trestle near Fisherville. Several persons have apparently been struck and killed by trains crossing the trestle, thanks in part to an acoustic anomaly that muffles the sound of approaching locomotives. The bridge thus acquired a grim reputation, enhanced by reports of a bipedal monster dwelling beneath it. Sometime in the 1940s—no source found during my research for this work offered specific dates—various witnesses reported sightings of the creature. Boy Scouts camped out near the trestle claimed that a nocturnal prowler screamed at them and pelted them with stones. Farmers in the vicinity have also blamed the beast for slaughtering their livestock.[17]

Descriptions of the Pope Lick Monster were inconsistent, including both a "goatman" and a "nondescript white, hair-covered creature." Sightings continued into the early 1950s, and interest was revived in 1988 by Ron Schildknecht's fictional film, *The Legend of the Pope Lick Monster*. Modern legends of the beast identify it as a vengeful fugitive from a circus freak show, or a hybrid monstrosity created when derailment of a cattle train mixed human and bovine remains.[18]

27.
Pope Lick's railroad trestle. *Image Courtesy of U.S. Fish & Wildlife Service*

The 1950s

Aside from Pope Lick Creek's conundrum, the 1950s produced a dozen Kentucky Bigfoot reports. The first, from Boone County in 1950, did not surface in print for another three decades. Writing in summer 1980, researcher John Daily referred to unspecified news clippings which, he says, described sightings of a large black creature that local residents nicknamed "Satan."[19]

Martin County produced two sightings in 1950, one from an un-named location in the county's southeast quadrant, and the other near

Beauty. In the first case, two teenage boys were fishing in a creek at dusk, when a hairy biped seven or eight feet tall approached from the woods. The youths fled, glancing back in time to see the creature take their fish. A local farmer subsequently told them that some unseen beast had killed and dismembered his dog. In the second incident, several children were frightened by a six-foot biped covered with hair "like a chimp's," which surprised them along the Tug River. The creature held a heavy stick in one hand and observed the children for several moments, before it turned and vanished.[20]

28.
The Tug River, site of a 1950 Bigfoot encounter. *Image Courtesy of U.S. Fish & Wildlife Service*

One night in 1951, three residents of Johnson County saw a huge bipedal creature near their rural home, between Van Lear and Wolfpen Hollow. As described by one witness, forty years later, the creature was nine or ten feet tall, covered in three-inch hair that "looked like copper." Peering through a window, it displayed large brown eyes and thin lips, but "never showed its teeth or made any kind of facial expression." After a moment's scrutiny, it turned and ran away into some woods behind the house.[21]

Sometime in October or December 1953 (reports differ), two boys playing outside their home in Liberty (Casey County) heard sounds "like two sticks being hit together" from the house next door. Approaching to investigate, they stopped short when a hairy biped rose to face them at a range of twenty-five feet. It was six to seven feet tall, mostly brown, with a "lighter vest" of gray. It bared long fangs in warning "like a dog would," flexing fingers tipped by thick, dirty nails. One witness says the creature held two sticks, using one like a hammer, driving the other to turn up loose soil in a presumed quest for food.[22]

Our next report comes from Pilgrim, in Martin County, near the Pike County line. The incident occurred in 1956 or 1957, but was not publicized until the early 1980s. Around the dinner hour, a Baptist minister and his wife observed an eight-foot-tall "hairy beast with red eyes" cross a field near their home and sit down on a tree stump. There it remained as night fell, while the witnesses cowered in their house, the preacher clutching a shotgun. At sunrise, the creature was gone.[23]

More details are available for the sighting recorded on May 15, 1957, from Wilson Ridge in Casey County. A farmer's wife was sewing a new dress for church, when her five-year-old son ran into the house, screaming about a "hairy man" outside. She saw nothing, but recognized the child's panic. For the remainder of that summer, he refused to go outside alone, and wept even when led by an adult. Until her death, the child's mother remained convinced that he had not been frightened by a human.[24]

Later in 1957, while riding with her grandmother and uncle between Beattyville and Belle Point, in Lee County, a witness identified only as "Phyllis" experienced a frightening nocturnal encounter. The uncle's truck was struggling along a muddy track, up White Ash Hill, when "something very large and frightening" dashed across the road, flinging holly branches from a nearby thicket toward the vehicle. The running assault was repeated time and again, over twenty-odd minutes, until the driver put his laboring truck in reverse and backed down the hill, out of range.[25]

The decade's penultimate sighting, vaguely dated from the "late 1950s," involved two teenage boys from Cary, in Bell County. While playing near an abandoned coal mine, they saw "a gray or white looking ape type animal on two legs," standing at the mouth of the shaft, one arm draped across a wooden beam some eight or nine feet off the ground. The boys fled to summon their parents, camped nearby, but the creature was gone when they returned.[26]

Early February 1959 brought a sighting from Covington, where a motorist crossing a bridge on the Licking River glimpsed "a thing on two legs, three or four times the size of a man and much bulkier." Shortly before that sighting, a Cincinnati trucker saw a "hulking creature" drag itself from the Ohio River and shamble off into the night.[27]

29.
Kentucky's Licking River. *Image Courtesy of U.S. Fish & Wildlife Service*

The 1960s

This decade produced seventeen specific Bigfoot sightings from ten counties. Casey County led the pack with six reports, but none are precisely dated.

The Casey County reports come to us from one of the Liberty youths who saw Bigfoot hammering sticks in the latter part of 1953, but none involve personal sightings. Instead, the still-unidentified witness reported various hearsay accounts spanning the years from 1960 to 1965. Two sightings from the former year were relayed to the witness years after the fact: One involved his ex-wife's cousin, one of three girls frightened by a creature that invaded the barn where they were playing; the other, related by the youth's employer at a local drive-in theater, described a Bigfoot that appeared to "sort of fold up and go under the water" beneath a rural bridge. The same employer claimed a second nocturnal sighting, while driving his projectionist home after work. Around the same time, a high-school classmate of the witness complained of a "hairy thing" that peered through her second-story bedroom window after nightfall. Finally, in 1965, a "hairy varmint" terrorized a coon hunter's dogs along Grove Ridge, while an unnamed state trooper was frightened off his nightly strolls along Goose Creek by "something" screaming in the forest.[28]

Multiple vague reports from a single anonymous source naturally inspire skepticism. On the other hand, they may reflect the subject's interest in Bigfoot, spawned by his childhood sighting, which encouraged him to collect more reports over time. The tardy filing of his stories was, apparently, occasioned by emergence of assorted Bigfoot websites in the 1990s.

Trimble County suffered a Bigfoot "flap" in June 1962, with two specific sightings detailed and others vaguely described. The string of incidents began with farmer Owen Pike (or Powell, in some reports) complaining that a six-foot-tall "gorilla" with arms that dangled to its knees had mauled his dogs. Soon afterward, on June 8, neighbor Siles McKinney claimed that the beast had killed one of his calves, leaving a barn wall scarred with claw marks and black hair littering the scene. Author John Keel reports that a necropsy on the calf attributed its death to blows on the head. Meanwhile, Keel says, "other animals in the area disappeared or were found mutilated."[29]

Sheriff Curtis Clem scoured the Trimble County woods with a posse, seven tracking dogs, and a helicopter—all in vain. Keel says that the searchers found footprints "like those of a giant dog," but descriptions of the creature gleaned from other unnamed witnesses were hopelessly confused. While some described "a gorilla or a big something-or-other with reddish hair," others struggled to sketch something "not quite a dog, a panther, or a bear." Small wonder, then, that chroniclers Colin and Janet Bord hedged while including the case on their list of Bigfoot sightings.[30]

One month after the Trimble County flap, Bigfoot surfaced in Rock-castle County, eighty miles to the southeast. Two teenage couples parked on lover's lane, outside Mount Vernon, were distracted from their beer and romance when a man-sized creature leaped onto the hood of their car and snarled at them through the windshield. It fled when the driver started his engine, and the teens raced back to town.[31]

Bart Nunnelly presents the next case, from Butler in Pendleton County, occurring sometime in 1964. Four youngsters were pedaling their bikes along the driveway toward a long-abandoned house, when a frightening creature emerged from the home's cellar door. It was "very tall, hairy, muscular, and resembled a gorilla in shape but much larger." The beast pursued them, snarling, for some fifty feet, then gave up the chase as they reached the main road.[32]

July 1964 brought reports of Sasquatch haunting a trash dump off U.S. Highway 36, in Grant County. Details are vague, but Bart Nunnelly claims multiple sightings of a seven-foot creature with "shiny eyes." Chaos ensued, with carloads of monster-hunters prowling the highway, firing at shadows—and sometimes at each other. Nunnelly reports that two teens suffered bullet wounds and police diverted fourteen carloads of gunmen in a single night, while sightings of the beast continued.[33] It seems curious that no other source logged the outbreak of "monster mania" prior to establishment of Nunnelly's Kentucky Bigfoot website in 2006, but reporting on the Sasquatch front has never been consistent or definitive.

Our next report, dating from 1966 or 1967, comes from Bell County—more specifically, "near Pineville, Brown's Creek, in Hen Holler, on Bugger Mountain." There is a Brownie's Creek in Bell County, located southwest of Miracle and four miles east of Pineville, but research for this work revealed no trace of Hen Holler or Bugger Mountain. The tale comes to us third-hand, from an unnamed correspondent, relating events that his father experienced as a young man, then told to his uncle and aunt. As finally reported to the GCBRO in June 1999, the witness was walking home at 2 or 3 a.m., when he heard branches snapping and saw a tall hairy biped nearby. The creature had "green glowing eyes that reflected red in the moonlight or something like that." The correspondent's grandmother subsequently reported a sighting of the same creature, at the same site.[34]

One night in 1968, Dr. Richard Young and companion Charles Denton saw Bigfoot walking along a road outside Murray, in Calloway County. No further details are available, and the story was not published until June 1977, when one witness told the *Nashville Banner*, "I haven't traveled that route since then."[35]

Our next story from the 1960s, not included in the decade's total, comes from Henderson County and overlaps the turn of the Twenty-first Century. According to Bart Nunnelly, who chronicled the case and launched a belated field expedition in December 2006, a series of Bigfoot sightings began around Hebbardsville and Reed, near the Green River, in 1968. Members of an unnamed family claimed multiple encounters with a green-eyed hairy biped at their rural home during 1968-1971, including one incident wherein the monster ripped their garage door from its moorings. A local farmer also blamed the beast(s) for killing and mutilating some of his livestock, by means of tearing off their lower jaws. Nunnelly ranks the district as "a very active" area for Bigfoot, as well as ABCs, water monsters, and unidentified flying objects. In December 2004, two stargazers atop "Negro Hill," on Pleasant Hill Road, watched a large biped uprooting corn stalks and nibbling their roots. While Nunnelly's 2006 investigation produced no physical evidence, he remains convinced of the creatures' existence, dubbing them "the Hebbardsville Hillbillies."[36]

Another third-hand report from the late 1960s involves the grandmother of an anonymous correspondent, who relayed the tale to Bart Nunnelly in January 2006. Details are sparse, but it appears that the witness—in her twenties at the time of the event—saw "a large ape creature" crossing Highway 196 near Jabez, in Russell County. A male passer-by may also have seen the creature.[37]

Finally, from October 1969, we have an atypical motorist's sighting from rural Livingston County. The unnamed witness was driving through woods at 11:30 p.m., when a four-foot-tall biped covered in "dull white" hair crossed the road in front of his vehicle, some twenty-five feet distant. The witness subsequently spoke to a local farmer's wife, who claimed three sightings of a similar beast on her property, but who provided no dates or details.[38]

The 1970s

Published accounts from the 1970s include thirty specific eyewitness sightings of Bigfoot-type creatures, plus five reported "flaps" involving multiple, unspecified sightings. Six additional cases involve reports of footprints, screams, or other evidence attributed to Bigfoot without actual sightings.

James Vincent, a self-described resident of Hendersonville, in Cumberland County, briefly describes his hunt for a large, white-haired creature which left fifteen-inch tracks and "a terrible smell" around Black Hollow, "near Bethpage" in "197?" He says the hunt was unsuccessful—and no wonder, since Kentucky has no towns named Bethpage or Hendersonville. There is a Black Hollow in Cumberland County (between Bakerton and Claywell), and a Henderson in Henderson County, but otherwise the details of Vincent's tale do not inspire confidence. Nonetheless, he assured Bart Nunnelly that the district "has [a] history of sightings and the creatures are known by locals there as 'Wild Woolly Bullies.'"[39]

Two unnamed Lewis County school bus drivers claimed sightings on the same morning in "197?," but the events were not reported until April 2003, by a relative of the witnesses. As described in that report, the first witness was driving his bus along Highway 59, cresting a hill near Vanceburg, when a humanoid figure covered in reddish-brown hair ran across the road. The second driver—a son of the initial witness—saw the same beast or its twin on another bus route, a half-mile distant from the first location. The relative who finally reported those encounters added that locals were accustomed to hearing "really scary sounds" from the forest, "like an ape and a chimpanzee [sic] mixed with human." Once, family members also found "weird looking hair" stuck to the screen door of an abandoned house, but "thought dogs had been going in or something."[40]

In summer 1971, an unseen "yowler" visited Pleasure Ridge Park, near Shively in Jefferson County. For several consecutive nights, "low moaning howls" disturbed the neighborhood and set dogs barking, but the beast behind the noise was never seen, nor were its footprints found. One local who recalls the incidents was ten years old at the time, and admits that his interpretation of the cries was influenced by release of a classic low-budget Bigfoot film, *The Legend of Boggy Creek*, in December 1972.[40]

30.
Film poster for *The Legend of Boggy Creek*. (A. HOWCO INTERNATIONAL PICTURES RELEASE)
Image Courtesy of Author's Collection

Two months before that film hit theaters nationwide, Logan County bow hunter Philip Wilkins had a close encounter with Bigfoot, six miles west of Russellville. Philips was stalking deer at night, beneath a full moon, when a bipedal creature seven or eight feet tall appeared before him in a soybean field. Its face was masked by shadow, but it had a short neck, arms that dangled almost to its knees, and Philips estimated that it weighed about 500 pounds. Philips fled to his Jeep and waited a week to return with heavier weapons, but he never saw the animal again.[41]

In summer 1973, three teenage boys camped out in a makeshift tent behind one's home, outside Berea in Madison County. They planned to sneak off and visit girlfriends, but got a late start on the journey, around 2 a.m. Their tryst was interrupted when a hairy white figure, seven or eight feet tall, frightened their leader into flight. Family members also reported visits from "the cruncher," an unseen prowler that snarled and made grinding sounds from the woods after nightfall, "like an animal munching on animal bones." Though never seen, its visits frightened humans and watchdogs alike. According to the primary witness, during this same period an unnamed local newspaper published reports of "unusual stuff" occurring at other rural homes.[42]

Autumn 1973 witnessed a monster flap in Clinton County, around Albany, where locals confronted an apparent family of unknown creatures. The presumed male was three feet tall when walking on all fours, but measured roughly six feet when it rose to walk on its hind legs. Some witnesses reported a black bushy tail, while others described a head "like an ape/human with a flat face and nose with large nostrils. Its ears were like mule ears and will perk up." Witness Rick Hall told author Loren Coleman that the beast had slaughtered two herds of pigs, along with a calf and a dog, leaping fences to attack its prey and taking massive ten-to-fifteen-foot strides. Coleman further reported that its tracks "were three-toed and distinctly manimal-like." The creature's mate and "cub" were proportionately smaller. Two different witnesses fired multiple gun-shots at the marauder, and while Charlie Stern claimed to have wounded the male, tracking it to a cave, he lost his nerve at the lair's threshold. Sightings ended thereafter, leaving the mystery unsolved.[43]

Two sightings come to us from 1974. The first, otherwise undated, occurred in Calloway County, where a young couple out for a late-night drive saw a bipedal creature six to seven feet tall cross the highway in front of their car. It was covered with "very dark fur, long and unkept [sic]," and walked with its shoulders "hunkered forward a bit." In September 1974, an eleven-year-old boy walking his dogs near Broughtentown (Lincoln County) met a "huge, long-haired, wide thing" in the woods. Boy and dogs "ran like the devil," but were not pursued. Six months later, the youth and his father found three humanoid footprints near the same location, and the witness claimed that his family "would hear things in the fall of the year ... [like] sounds of trees crashing and loud noises."[44]

The year 1975 produced at least three sightings, and possibly five. (Witnesses were unsure of the year in two cases.) The first report, from Bart Nunnelly's website, says that a "large, hairy Bigfoot" was seen near Hamlin, in Calloway County, but offers no further details. On August 9, a young boy camping with his family at Nolin River Lake, near Leitchfield (Grayson County), saw a grayish-brown "man thing" crouched in some nearby shrubbery. The witness waited thirty years to report his sighting, at which time he recalled the date but not the year, narrowing the range to "1975-1977." On September 15, 1975, an eight-foot hairy prowler with foul body odor distracted two rural Breathitt County residents from a nocturnal television program. Adding insult to injury, the beast left a pile of feces eight inches wide and five inches high in the yard.[46]

Another sighting, reported by "John D." in 1997 but dating from summer "1975-76," issued from the Pritchett farm, on Old Henderson Road in Henderson County. The witness was a young teenager on the afternoon when he and a friend saw a biped seven or eight feet tall, which "wobbled" as it walked. Its hair was light tan, thinner on the "human type face" than on its head and shoulders. John D. only saw the creature's upper body, but estimated its weight at 350 pounds. He also told Bart Nunnelly that he believed the beast "was trying to communicate telepathically," which engendered "a very bad feeling."[47]

31.
Nolin River Lake, site of a 1975 Bigfoot report.
Image Courtesy of U.S. Army Corps of Engineers

John D. was only one of Henderson County's witnesses, as Spottsville suffered a full-scale Bigfoot flap in 1975. Bart Nunnelly reports that John's mother and sister saw three different creatures—a "good" one with white hair, a brown "evil" one, and another that turned up dressed in "an old, beat-up hat and a tattered shirt." The siege continued for eleven months, during which time the family saw one beast "disappear into thin air on three separate occasions." Despite such oddities, Nunnelly considers John D. "a reliable witness." Earlier reports of the "Spottsville Monster," such as that published in the Owensburg *Messenger-Inquirer* on February 9, 1977, contained no substantive details. Nunnelly's endorsement of John D. may be influenced by his own family's reported encounters with the "Spottsville Monster," beginning in 1975 and continuing into January 1976. During that veritable siege of their rural farm, the Nunnellys found eight dogs, a pig, and a goat mutilated in nearby woods, while neighbors fired futile gunshots at the resident "hairy feller" who harassed them.[48]

Spring of 1976 brought three reported primate sightings from the neighborhood of Pembroke, in Christian County. All occurred at night, near isolated rural homes, with five witnesses involved. Descriptions of the beast pegged its height around six feet, noting broad shoulders and glowing green eyes.[49]

The action switched to Clark County that summer, when five brothers went cycling near Winchester. A description of the area, provided by witness "Joe H." in 1999, refers to a nonexistent "Booneboro River" (probably Boone Creek), and to the town of Richmond, located fifteen miles south of Winchester, in neighboring Madison County. Whatever the precise location, Joe H. recalled his brother Donald's panic at seeing "a hairy monster" in the woods. Donald H. subsequently sketched the creature, which resembled drawings of Bigfoot seen by Joe H. after their family moved to Washington.[50]

The GCBRO website includes a report from "rural Ohio County," dating from summer 1976. However, the unnamed witness describes the event as occurring near Panther Creek (Daviess County), between Whitesville and Pelville (in Hancock County). The occasion was a visit to retrieve parts from a junk car, long abandoned at a rural farm. While thus engaged, the witness heard sounds from the nearby woods and saw a biped he described as "big, black, and hairy, with lighter patches that could have been mud or dirt." The man fled without taking a closer look, later telling the GCBRO, "I will regret that for the rest of my life."[51]

Bigfoot visited Fort Knox in October 1976, frightening a young soldier who met the beast during a pre-dawn training exercise. The witness described it as approximately six-foot-five inches tall, standing in waist-high grass that obscured its lower body. Headlights on a passing army truck revealed a beast covered with hair whose hue and texture matched that of an Irish setter. It had no visible neck, but the soldier noted its "black or very dark eyes." Overall, he found the creature "humanlike, yet not."[52]

Our next witness, an unidentified Simpson County policeman, saw "a large hairy animal" crossing a road at night, in January 1977. Louisville residents Michael Johnson and James Moorhatch advised author John Green of other Simpson County sightings, but no details have been published.[53]

Another report on file dates from July 1977, and comes from the mountainous region near Chavies, in Perry County. Witness "Rick S." was spending time at his uncle's secluded home, ten miles north of Hazard, when Bigfoot disrupted a late-night television program. The first alarm came from a pony corralled outside, prompting the witness and a cousin to arm themselves with frog gigs, expecting to confront a bobcat. Instead, they met a biped seven to nine feet tall and "as wide as two men standing shoulder to shoulder." It fled, leaving tracks that were visible next morning, where the beast had jumped across a nearby creek.[54]

Around the same time, a different creature appeared at Jeffersontown, in Jefferson County. This one was white, and looked "ferocious" enough to frighten the unnamed motorist-witness who fled at top speed. A couple parked outside of Louisville were interrupted by a white Bigfoot, one night in September 1977, and July's Jefferson County witness claimed another sighting of the same thing, or its twin, in October, three miles from the site of the first incident. Years later, he told GCBRO investigators that Jefferson County residents referred to their local nightstalker as "a sheepman."[55]

Incidents attributed to Bigfoot continued in 1978, beginning in western Kentucky. No sightings accompanied the discovery of large, humanoid footprints at Lake Barkley, in Trigg County, but July brought a disturbing report from Livingston County, to the northwest. Teenager Jan Thompson was visiting relatives at Grand Rivers, near Kentucky Lake, when a bipedal creature tried to snatch her cousin Joe from his dirt bike, leaving bloody scratches on his leg in "a definite wide pattern of a paw print." Howling noises followed, from the woods, before a monstrous creature resembling a Hollywood werewolf emerged from the trees. According to Thompson, "it resembled a Bigfoot...except for the pointed ears and longer snout and claws that it had." The children fled into their house, pursued by the beast, which smashed a bedroom window, then fled when Thompson's aunt returned from a trip to the grocery store, sounding her Cadillac's horn. Thompson's subsequent Internet writings refer to legends of "dogmen" in Livingston County, and throughout the nearby Land Between the Lakes.[56] (See Chapter 6)

32.
Lake Barkley, where
large footprints ap-
peared in 1978 and
1981. *Image Courtesy
of U.S. Fish & Wildlife
Service*

Owensboro, in Daviess County, proved hazardous for Bigfoot in August 1978. Witness Larry Nelson, his brother, and two friends pursued a
biped 8 to 10 feet tall from Fairview Drive into some nearby woods and
cornered it near a pond, where Nelson fired three close-range shots from
a .45-caliber pistol. The creature then escaped, apparently unharmed,
leaving behind a smell "like decomposing bodies" and footprints measuring 14 to 16 inches long, by 6 to 7 inches wide. It may be that this
incident excited the authors Colin and Janet Board so much that they
inadvertently listed the event twice with slightly altered details in their
published chronology of Bigfoot sightings.[57] Bigfoot ambled eastward in
August 1978, to surface at Powell County's Natural Bridge State Park, in
the Daniel Boone National Forest. Ten-year-old witness "Matt H." was
hiking near his family's camp on August 15, when he noticed an "awful
smell" and spied "the biggest footprint I'd ever seen" in a muddy stream
bed. Glancing up from the "enormous" track, he glimpsed a bipedal
creature covered with "shiny, like greasy hair," watching him from the
nearby woods. The creature fled immediately, as Matt H. ran to fetch his
stepfather and uncle. In retrospect, he told BFRO investigators that the
single footprint "easily doubled my step dad's size 10½ foot."[58]

Two days after that incident, on August 17, witness "B.A." heard a
shrieking cry "like nothing I had ever heard before" at his farm outside
Campbellsville, in Taylor County. Its source was still unknown in August
1988, when the eerie call was repeated, once again frightening the witness and his wife. The incidents may be irrelevant to Bigfoot, since both
witnesses note that "many of the locals had seen a black panther in the
hills over the years," yet they reported the events to the BFRO's website
in October 2001.[59]

Autumn 1978 brought a sighting from Henry County, northwest of
Frankfort. Witness "K.D." and his brother were eating dinner at their

rural home, near Lockport, when horses in the barn began "making a lot of noise, kicking and nickering." Sent by their parents to investigate, the boys saw "a very tall, hairy creature" standing outside the barn. The beast was tall enough that a nearby hitching post came only to its knees. Subsequent events around the farm included "a sort of screaming" sound from the woods, one night in 1979, and an undated discovery of eighteen-inch footprints at Hances Branch, "so fresh [that] water was just starting to seep into them." Family members recorded the strange woodland cries and played them for a game warden who "said they were mountain lions mating"—an oddity in itself, since Kentucky's cougars are presumed to be extinct. K.D.'s grandfather also claimed that "something threw rocks at him one day, large rocks that were [thrown] with great force." Bart Nunnelly reports that Henry County "has [a] history of similar phenomenon," but he provides no details.[60]

Kentucky's last Bigfoot sighting of 1978 occurred three days before Christmas, when flood waters threatened Paintsville, in Johnson County. Resident Shirley Elkins sat by her radio all night, overlooking a nearby graveyard. Late that evening, neighborhood dogs began barking, then Elkins felt a vibration "like hands shaking the house." Glancing up, she recalls, "All I could see was fur against the window." The shaggy prowler soon retreated, revealing itself as "a human-looking creature." It rampaged through the cemetery, shaking trees and ripping up shrubs, before it vanished into the night. Elkins's husband had grappled with a hungry primate back in 1944, but on this occasion he and the home's other occupants saw nothing.[61]

Early March 1979 produced multiple sightings of a night-prowling "ape-man," logged by motorists traversing the Pennyrile Parkway in Christian County. No further details are available, and the next published report dates from June, when some unseen, howling creature shook Vicki Jones's trailer in rural Boone County. The last sighting for 1979, otherwise undated, comes from Flat Lick, in Knox County, where four young boys saw a seven-foot biped cross their yard. It was, they recalled years later, "apparently male, no breast[s], [with a] muscular build." The decade's final sighting, dated vaguely from the "late 1970s," also involved four children. These were girls, bicycling in Lyon County's Land Between the Lakes, who heard "crashing sounds" in the woods, "like a car being dropped to the ground," which they later blamed on Bigfoot.[62]

The 1980s

This decade produced twenty-seven specific sightings of unknown bipedal creatures, plus seven incidents involving strange sounds or footprints that witnesses attributed to Bigfoot. Another case, listed by the GCBRO as a Kentucky sighting, is omitted here because the witness clearly described the creature heard and seen as a "black panther." Four of the sightings involve atypical white-haired bipeds.[63]

A few months after Vicki Jones was frightened by a shrieking night-walker in Boone County, Bigfoot returned to visit other members of her family on March 31, 1980. Jackie Jones and David Stultz were preparing for bed at 12:30 a.m., in the same trailer Vicki had formerly occupied, when they and son Jason heard a noise "like a combination of a lion and elephant roar" outside. Next came a violent jerking on the trailer, as someone or something tried to lift it from its foundation. Peering outside, they saw a black flat-faced creature approximately 5 feet tall and "2-3 feet wide," weighing an estimated 300 pounds. Stultz rushed outside with a shotgun and fired several blasts, whereupon the creature fled, running on all fours, and dived into a nearby river. Four police officers answered the call, but they found no tracks or other physical evidence.[64]

September 1980 produced the next Bigfoot sighting, published by Bart Nunnelly twenty years after the fact. It occurred in Harlan County, where an unnamed witness saw a large biped cross Highway 1137. The beast had long arms, "human-looking hands," and a head described as "long and wider at the bottom," with a crest of stiff, "nappy" hair on top.[65]

Confusion surrounds the next sighting, reported on October 4, 1980. Colin and Janet Bord place it near Maysville, while Bart Nunnelly and the BFRO claim that it occurred outside May's Lick (misspelled "Mayslick" by both sources). In either case, it was in Mason County—as was the next sighting, on October 10. The first case involved witnesses Charles Fulton and Anna Mae Saunders, described in some reports as "the Fulton family." Fulton and Saunders were watching television when loud noises from the front porch distracted them, and they beheld a seven-foot, 400-pound monster with glowing pink eyes and a coat of white hair. The hair on its head was longer, resembling "a horse's mane." Fulton fired 2 shots at the beast from a .22-caliber pistol, whereupon it fled into the night.[66]

Six days later, at Maysville's Central Shopping Center, Bigfoot chased a woman around her car, then abruptly gave up the pursuit and departed. No description survives to tell us if it was the same white beast seen on October 4. That same night, or the next (reports differ), J.L. Tumey was watching television at his home in rural Fleming County, when a racket on his back porch brought him outside with gun in hand. Tumey beheld a tall, dark figure fleeing into the night and emptied his pistol in panic, later telling reporters, "It was very dark, so I really could not tell exactly what it was. It stood up like a man, but it was so dark, about all I could see was a huge shadow. It made a thumping noise as it ran away." After the prowler escaped, Tumey found his outdoor freezer opened and frozen chicken scattered about. "Unusual white hairs" clung to the freezer, while "impressions" resembling large footprints marked the yard. The next morning, Tumey found more tracks in a nearby gully, estimating their length at twelve to fourteen inches, but BFRO investigators report that "the prints were not clear enough to establish whether it was a man's print."[67]

Four weeks after the Tumey skirmish, on November 5, 1980, an Alabama truck driver stopped to pick up an apparent hitchhiker on U.S. Highway 68, west of Maysville, between 4 and 5 a.m. The driver, identified only as "N.C.," prepared to greet the stranger but was "terribly shaken" when a closer look revealed a seven-foot-tall ape-like creature covered with white hair. The trucker sped away, then used his CB radio to contact police, asking if a local zoo had lost one of its apes.[68]

Our next report comes from Carter County, where an unnamed witness settled with his family in 1980, on a farm six miles from Grayson. Two months after their arrival, the witness began hearing sounds after nightfall "that made me a little uncomfortable but not frightened." His report to the BFRO, filed in 2001, dates the events from winter of "1980-1983," adding that "these things occurred during the rest of the year too." The witness also reported "a few things that wasn't what I call natural forest happenings," such as trees uprooted and stacked to form "teepee structures." He claimed no Bigfoot sightings, per se, but on several occasions saw "eyes that looked blood red, and another time green, as they were looking at me from the low underbrush at night." Two of the witness's children claimed a biped sighting, sometime in 1997-98, but furnished no useful details.[69]

In mid-January 1981, the weekly *Cadiz Record* reported discovery of oversized humanoid footprints around Lake Barkley. Local authorities declared the case a hoax, but Bart Nunnelly claims a discovery of similar tracks at the same place in 1978, deeming the fraud "an extremely determined one [by someone] who took the trouble to ramble through briars and thickets where no man could easily go."[70]

Repeat monster witness Jan Thompson is next to weigh in, with a dramatic sighting vaguely dated from "the early 1980s," coming once again from the Land Between the Lakes. The incident in question occurred when Thompson worked at a gas station near Grand Rivers and the Kentucky Dam, in Livingston County. On that occasion, "about twenty-two years" prior to 2007, Thompson claims that two unnamed policemen arrived at the station "shaken beyond description" by the slaughter of three tourists at a nearby campground. Thompson describes the crime scene in graphic terms, without having seen it herself, and reports that the bodies were slashed by "well-defined claws" and "mordantly long incisors." The bite marks were "much larger than any mountain lion" [sic], and investigators allegedly recovered long grayish-brown hairs at the scene. The case presumably remains unsolved, but who can say? Thompson avers that it "was kept hush hush, and a sacred silence was demanded on all those involved," to prevent spreading panic.[71]

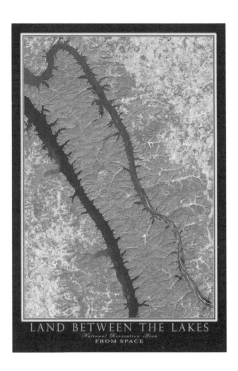

33.
Kentucky's Land Between the Lakes, as seen from outer space. *Image Courtesy of National Aeronautics and Space Administration*

And, if that was not strange enough, Thompson logged another personal encounter with some unknown biped on December 24, 1983, while driving near Sturgis, in Union County. This creature—which Thompson and Bart Nunnelly dub "the Sturgis vampire"—resembled a gaunt nude man, except for its bestial head and "sprigs" of long hair dangling from its elbows and back. The thing's face, framed by long tangled hair, reminded Thompson of an African-American's, except for its pale skin, glowing red eyes, and long fangs. Blood smeared the creature's lips and hands. Despite her shock, Thompson noted the figure's muscles ("resembling finely chiseled Italian marble") and a painful-looking rash on its genitalia.[72]

Meanwhile, a more mundane primate appeared to two fishermen in rural Union County, one evening in June 1982. The creature was "big, black, and hairy," observed as it descended from the branches of a tree.

The following year, four Kentucky campers saw a "gentle giant" more than seven feet tall, watching their tents from an estimated distance of 100 yards.[73]

Two reports are presently on file from 1984. The first, from the vicinity of Lost Creek (Breathitt County), involved the January discovery of child-sized footprints on the ice spanning a frozen stream. The tracks measured eight inches long, by three or four inches wide. Bart Nunnelly writes that no children were reported missing in the district, and suggests that the tracks were made by a "possible juvenile Bigfoot." Four months later, a five-man hunting party in Owen County tracked "a large, hairy bipedal creature" that had raided local farms. Its trail led to a cave, which the men explored, but they found it empty, with no alternate exits.[74]

Our sole case from 1985 represents a nocturnal sighting in rural Scott County, published twenty years after the fact. Four passengers in a car saw a "tall, dark, hairy man-like thing" framed in their headlights. It was eight or nine feet tall and "in no hurry" as it "walked over" a six-foot roadside fence without aid of its dangling hands. The witnesses described reflective eyes and "a strong, indescribable odor" reminiscent of severe flatulence.[75]

The year 1986 offers no sightings, but a case of supposed Bigfoot vocalization has been widely reported from Coal Harbor Hill, in Perry County. Witness Carlen Dixon and a friend were walking on a rural road in June or July (reports differ), around 2 a.m., when they heard a scream that "definitely was NOT human, but it sounded like no animal I had ever heard. It was simultaneously high-pitched and growling; it was very strange." A second, longer shriek followed, lasting for six or seven seconds. Subsequently, Dixon heard recordings of a supposed Bigfoot's call online, reporting that it "is EXACTLY the sound we heard that night."[76]

Four teens were driving aimlessly through southern Jefferson County, one night in summer 1987, when "a very loud and very long scream" from the woods interrupted their cruising. Suspecting a prank, they stopped their car and shouted curses at the unseen shrieker, then heard sounds of "something big" rushing toward them through the forest. They panicked and fled without glimpsing the prowler, but later reported the incident to the GCBRO's website as a possible Bigfoot encounter.[77]

Around the same time, a similar event occurred near Burbanks Lake, in Henderson County, at a site nicknamed "Spook Hill." Two local men were fishing on the lake at night, but every time they tried to land their boat, the woods echoed with heavy footsteps and snapping branches nearby. Frightened, they spent the night afloat and were "allowed" to leave at sunrise, when their tormentor retreated. Intrigued, the brother of one witness led five friends to Burbanks Lake for an experiment—

and they, too, heard "a terrifyingly loud commotion" that put them to flight after sundown.[78]

The year 1988 produced four Bigfoot sighting reports, regrettably sparse on details. Bart Nunnelly says that an artifact hunter glimpsed a six-foot biped near Reed, "close to the Stanley County line," but neither Kentucky nor its seven border states have a county by that name. Another Bigfoot frightened two Indiana deer hunters out of Union County's Higginson-Henry Wildlife Management Area. Chad Askins and a friend were drinking beer beside a creek in rural Ohio County, that summer, when they were scared away by a hairy creature "over ten feet tall." Finally, two Pike County witnesses observed a "smokey-gray" creature that walked on two legs but dropped to all fours when it ran.[79]

No date beyond the "late 1980s" is supplied for two more cases, reported by Bart Nunnelly. In the first incident, from Pilgrim in Martin County, an eight-foot-tall red-eyed monster surprised two nocturnal fishermen on their way home. They were "saved" by dropping their catch, which the creature paused to consume, but sunrise found a neighbor's dog dismembered and partially devoured. Searchers found "extremely big" humanoid tracks near the carcass. In the second case, three Lawrence County hunters were frightened when a seven-foot biped covered with long white hair approached their car, outside Louisa. Before fleeing the scene, they noted that the creature walked "in a peculiar manner," with its arms extended forward.[80]

The 1990s

This decade produced forty-three specific Bigfoot sightings from thirty-one counties, plus one with no location specified and a vague report of "several" sightings in Crittenden County. The list begins with three cases dated only from "the early 1990s."

The first two incidents occurred around Geneva, in Henderson County. In one case, a hunter fled his deer stand after glimpsing a an eight-foot biped frizzy-haired giant. Subsequently, four night-riding teens were parked beside an unmapped lake known as the "Genny Hole," when they heard "a terrible scream" from the lake's far side, followed by sounds of "something huge" diving into the water and swimming toward them. They fled without seeing the swimmer, and later told their story to Bart Nunnelly. Two teenage hikers also found "very large" humanoid footprints in snow outside Kimper (Pike County), in a district dotted with abandoned coal mines.[81]

Perennial witness Jan Thompson provides our first dated report, from Marshall County, during April 1990. While employed as a courier for the

World Wide Delivery Service, Thompson approached a rural home and noticed deer in flight, accompanied by flocks of birds, fleeing as if in panic from a forest fire. Seconds later, a hulking figure with "a thick furry outline," standing "eight to nine feet tall, at least," emerged from the forest and uttered a "hideous sound." Although shaken, Thompson completed her delivery. The parcel's recipient admitted that his livestock was frequently "spooked" by strange sounds from the woods, and he described the disappearance of a neighbor's hunting dog, presumably snatched by Bigfoot. One version of the story places Thompson's sighting between 10:30 a.m. and noon, while another places it between 1 and 3p.m.[82]

Five alleged Bigfoot encounters are on file for 1991, four of them collected and reported by Bart Nunnelly. One of those—relayed by "Steve" of Breckenridge County—is hearsay, repeating a tale of a "very strange sound, a type of scream or something," heard by his late father outside Cloverport. Screams also featured in two other cases where creatures were seen. In July, a father and son heard "a loud screeching roar" from the woods near their Lewisburg farm (Logan County), then saw a "tall, large, hairy... animal of some sort" fleeing on two legs. Two months later, near Ashland in Boyd County, a pair of unnamed hikers heard a "deafening scream-roar-growl," then saw a "massive" long-haired creature running toward them "somewhat [on] all fours." It stopped nearby and rose on its hind legs, whereupon they judged it to be "at least sixteen feet tall." They escaped in their car, while "the creature apparently chased them." Next morning, they returned and discovered "rather weird looking tracks or footprints."[83]

Before those startling events, in May 1991, an unnamed motorist reported a hairy biped seven to eight feet tall, ambling along an unspecified "north-south highway in central Kentucky." Autumn 1991 brought reports from Cynthiana (Harrison County), where two witnesses saw a three-foot-tall biped with a "cat-like/monkey face" cross the road in front of their car. In November 1992, two Lawrence County hunters saw a larger beast moving with "long steps, walking fast, very much like a human." The latter Bigfoot left a pile of loose feces containing grass and long black hairs, which was not preserved for study.[84]

The year 1993 produced four Bigfoot reports. In January, two sisters traveling between Mayfield and Wickliffe (Ballard County) reported a roadside sighting of an eight-foot creature with "human features, especially the eyes." Six months later, a Madison County hiker met a seven-foot apelike creature on Bear Mountain. October brought a sighting from Anderson County, where two hunters saw an eight-foot biped covered in long brown hair. Two unnamed Christian County witnesses also saw a gray-haired, red-eyed creature poised beside a rural road, one night in 1993, but could not recall the specific date.[85]

In Lincoln County, sometime during "1993-94," two children found "a big footprint" in mud but it was not preserved. Two sightings from 1994 boast multiple witnesses. In the first case, eight nocturnal hunters saw a bipedal creature seven or eight feet tall, standing beside an old mining road near Virgie, in Pike County. It left one four-toed footprint in roadside mud, measuring fifteen or sixteen inches long. In the second case, a Pike County couple driving on Highway 168, between 12:30 and 1 a.m., glimpsed a biped seven to eight feet tall, with "dark brown to black hair all over its body."[86]

The remainder of the decade produced twenty-five reports, including four from 1995, three in 1996, two in 1997, eleven from 1998, one from "1997-98," and three from 1999. Unfortunately, two of the 1995 reports claim only unknown noises; a third is hearsay, its second-hand source closing with the remark "True or false, who knows?"; and only one involves a first-person sighting. The last event occurred in Hopkins County, near White Plains, on November 7, in an area locally known as "Lonesome Woods." Witness J.T. Oglesby and three fellow campers were roused by a sound "like a siren except...very loud." Some ninety minutes later, one of the men went to relieve himself and saw an eight-foot creature drinking from a nearby stream. His friends rushed over with a light and saw the "silhouette of a very large creature" retreating.[87]

Incidents from 1996 included a sighting by two mussel poachers at Lake Barkley State Park, and a woman's moonlight sighting of a creature nine or ten feet tall near Uniontown (Union County). Bart Nunnelly places the latter incident near "the infamous 'Slack Farm,'" which Nunnelly investigated personally near decade's end. While prowling the area, Nunnelly found mutilated carcasses of several pigs, freshly killed without being eaten. He saw no monsters, but reported a sensation of being watched.[88]

On July 12, 1997, witness Harry Hardin logged a daylight sighting from the south fork of the Cumberland River, near a point called Devils Jump in McCreary County. He watched "something strange" cross the river, concluding that it "was not a canoe, person, or a bear." The bipedal creature stood waist-deep at midstream, prompting a guess that it was seven or eight feet tall. Later, some fifteen miles away, Hardin found "a dome structure made from sticks" which he believed might be the creature's nest. Three months later, a father and son driving near Shady Grove, in Crittenden County, saw a creature six-foot-ten inches tall beside a forest road. In a final sighting for the year, a teenage resident of Rockhold (Whitley County) was cutting trees near her rural home when she met a biped eight feet tall and four feet wide across the chest, with large hands, an "almost human face," and reddish-brown hair six to eight inches long.[89]

34.
Part of the Cumberland
River, scene of a 1997
Bigfoot sighting. *Image
Courtesy of U.S. Fish &
Wildlife Service*

In January 1998 several more unnamed witnesses claimed contact with a red-eyed biped near Shady Grove in Crittenden County. Two months later, witness "Doug" heard strange sounds near his Firebrick home (Lewis County) and found broken trees in the woods. Members of the Ohio Bigfoot Search Group visited Doug's property on March 5 and reported hearing "two sounds that we know Bigfoot makes." August 1998 brought a report from Ashland (Boyd County), where a motorist and her son saw Bigfoot cross a twenty-foot-wide road in two strides, around 2:45 a.m. On September 10, two Louisville joggers in Jefferson County Memorial Forest saw a brown-haired primate seven to eight feet tall, weighing an estimated 400-plus pounds. Two other sightings, neither precisely dated, involved the nocturnal sighting of a "large hairy animal with glowing red eyes" near a Graves County gravel pit, outside Mayfield, and a two-witness sighting of a "dark figure" eight and a half feet tall near Lake Cumberland, in Russell County.[90]

35.
Lake Cumberland.
*Image Courtesy of U.S.
Fish & Wildlife Service*

The decade closed with four sightings in 1999, though two of those are vaguely dated and one may actually have occurred in 2000. On July 14, while camped out overnight in Knox County, a group of berry pickers were wakened by crashing sounds and saw a foul-smelling bipedal figure seven to eight feet tall "knocking down small trees." A second sighting in July, at Lake Barkley in Lyon County, involved a slender six-foot hairy biped with "an hourglass figure," presumed to be female, which "ran like a human." On August 4, one of the Russell County witnesses from 1998 saw another Bigfoot near Lake Cumberland. A Henderson County motorist saw two "very big" bipeds in a bean field beside Highway 60, near Baskett, but could not recall the date. Finally, a driver traveling through Grant County on Interstate 75, en route from Lexington to Winchester, glimpsed a large upright creature in autumn "1999 or 2000."[91]

Twenty-First-Century Sightings

At press time for this book, the new century had produced fifty-two alleged Kentucky Bigfoot encounters. Thirteen of those events were limited to strange sounds, smells, or suggestive trace evidence, but the remaining thirty-nine were purported eyewitness sightings of large unknown creatures.

The decade began with four reports from 2000. On May 1, an Eddyville motorist narrowly avoided striking a "huge beast" with a "human" face and "body almost ape like." It saw him off with a "low but loud growling sound." Three months later, a couple fishing by night near Mortons Gap (Hopkins County) heard a large shrieking creature slap their nearby pickup truck several times. Early September produced Joann Carter's Harlan County sighting of a biped more than eight feet tall, which left hairs dangling from a tree limb. Researcher Bobbie Short says that Carter "has this hair sample but is unwilling to let a scientist examine it as proof of her sighting." In November, an Anderson County witness reported "the scariest scream I have ever heard," but did not see the thing responsible.[92]

On January 4, 2001, witness "M.L." reported a frightening encounter in the Greenup County woods near Raceland. The nocturnal sighting of an eight-foot, 450-pound biped prompted M.L. to "about [soil] my pants," but he still had the presence of mind to photograph the creature's large humanoid footprints. February brought two sightings from Louellen, in Harlan County, where motorists saw a seven-foot biped prowling along Highway 119. Early spring produced a report of some unknown creature howling around Lake Barkley State Park, in Trigg County. On November 7, a nine-foot "cross between a monkey and a bear" startled a driver outside Hazard (Perry County) and left twenty-inch footprints behind. Later in the same month, a Lincoln County hunter saw a strange beast near Crab Orchard. It "looked like a bear when it walked on all fours," then stood upright and "threw [a] stick like a man."[93]

36.
Lake Barkley State Park. *Image Courtesy of Kentucky Department of Parks*

Our next sighting, by witness "Joey" and a friend, occurred near Pineville (Bell County) sometime in 2002. The beast was "big, with dark fur, walking on two feet."

Witness "Jeremiah" and four companions logged an encounter near Maysville, sometime in late 2002 or early 2003. The five were returning from Germantown on Highway 435, around 11 p.m., when they saw a hairy biped six to seven feet tall standing beside the road. Jeremiah and his brother subsequently saw the same creature or its twin, running along Clyde T. Barbour Highway in the same vicinity. On that occasion, they noted its black fur, red eyes, and "stringy hair longer on the shoulders that looked like it was wet."[94]

On February 20, 2003, a motorist driving near Pine Knot, in Mc-Creary County, saw a gray-haired, seven-foot creature "rant[ing] around like it was angry" on the shoulder of Highway 92. Before the witness fled, he saw the beast wave its arms and clutch its head with both hands, while glaring at his vehicle with reddish eyes.[95]

June 2003 produced Bigfoot sightings from Kenton and Barren Counties. The first, on June 24, involved two players at an unspecified "frisbee golf course" in a wooded district. A smell like rotting flesh preceded the appearance of a nine-foot apelike creature that emitted high-pitched shrieks and advanced with "a hunched over kind of skip" while the witnesses ran to their car. Six days later, at the Diamond Caverns Resort near Cave City, a family of four heard loud screams from the woods like "that of a women being brutalized," which they attributed to Bigfoot.[96]

37.
Diamond Caverns Resort. *Image Courtesy of Kentucky Department of Parks*

In July 2003, while hunting ginseng in the woods near Blaine (Lawrence County), a husband and wife heard thrashing noises in the underbrush, then saw a bipedal creature covered with reddish-brown hair, six to seven feet tall and four feet wide at the shoulders. The male witness carried a rifle, but did not fire because "it looked like a man to me." Watching the creature from twenty to thirty feet in broad daylight, the witnesses described its face as "flat like a person or a monkey [sic]." Retreating, it ran on two legs "like a man covered with hair."[97]

Our last report for 2003 is vague at best. Two unnamed witnesses near Ashland logged a daylight sighting of a "tall brown upright thing," six or seven feet tall, crossing a highway in daylight. While they recalled the time—5 p.m.—the date eluded them.[98]

The year 2004 produced five sightings, with the first occurring near Stanton (Powell County) on April 20. While walking past a rural garbage dump at 2:30 a.m., the unnamed witness heard splashing in a nearby river and observed "a big shape" in the water. He mistook the creature for a bear until it stood upright, revealing a coat of "long shaggy hair." The beast had "a long head, not really pointed, but sort of cone shaped," and it "stank, really horrible."[99]

Two months later, on a June night in Trigg County, two anonymous Bigfoot researchers claimed a sighting on the property of a private hunting club. They were touring the land by night, in an off-road vehicle, when their headlights illuminated amber eyes, elevated seven or eight feet above the forest floor. They saw no more of the creature, but estimated that its huge eyes were "slightly smaller than the diameter of a snuff can." Around the same time, a McCreary County couple reported hearing strange calls like a peacock's cry near Parkers Lake. Sometime before year's end, two members of the Garcia family saw a hairy biped prowling outside their home at Cold Spring, in Campbell County.[100]

On January 21, 2005 an unnamed witness saw a peculiar biped at his home in Spencer County. The two-toned beast was roughly eight feet tall, and while its upper body was covered with brown hair, its "muscular/toned but much skinnier lower body" was "beige, possibly hairless." The witness reported his daylight sighting to the GCBRO's website on January 31, adding sparse details of four previous Bigfoot encounters during 2002-04. Aside from those sightings, he claimed multiple incidents of shrieking in the woods that sounded "like a human child howling."[101]

Three sightings from July 2005 round out the year's reports. Adam Candler was driving near Spottsville on July 14, when he saw a "large, dark object" crouched in a ditch beside Green River Road. As he approached, it rose to a height of eight feet and fled on two legs. Nine days later, a nocturnal hiker saw a Bigfoot with "human-like eyes and a bad smell" chasing deer beside an unnamed Warren County lake. Before the month ended, a Trigg County motorist saw a huge biped standing beside State Route 164. Rocking on its heels, it was "at least ten feet tall and covered with thick black hair." According to the witness, it "looked just like a big old hairy man standing there—more like a human than a gorilla."[102]

The year 2006 produced fifteen sightings, beginning with an odd case from January. Witness "Mark" was fascinated by Bigfoot, and in fact was driving to meet a researcher in Tennessee when the sighting occurred, though he remains uncertain as to whether it happened in Stewart or Trigg County. The creature framed in his headlights was "roughly the size of a big cat," but had no tail or visible ears on its "rather small head." It crawled on all fours, with "a lizard-like motion," and Mark concluded that it was not a primate at all, though his friends maintain that it was "a juvenile Bigfoot."[103]

May brought three reports, the first involving witness "Matt" and three companions near Morehead, in Rowan County. Moonlight and headlights revealed a seven-foot animal "covered in black shaggy hair that hung on him." On May 24, near Inez in Martin County, three campers were disturbed by groaning that "went on for hours," prior to their discovery of an eight-foot creature snoring in the woods nearby. It woke at their approach and "took off hastily," running on two legs. One day later, still in Martin County, fifteen campers heard screams and saw a creature eight or nine feet tall, with large teeth and "piercing red eyes." Pistol shots drove it back from the camp.[104]

The action continued in June 2006, with three sightings from as many counties. Three campers near Ermine (Letcher County) saw a seven-foot primate at 1 a.m. on June 4, while another beast frightened motorist "Rick" outside Independence, in Kenton County, three nights later. On June 27, two youths lighting fireworks in a rock quarry outside Mount Vernon (Rockcastle County) saw a brown-haired creature of similar size watching them from 100 yards distant. On July 2, a biped eight or nine feet tall lobbed heavy stones at witness "Josh" in the Bon Harbor Hills, near Owensboro (Daviess County). One week later, a shrieking creature that "looked like an ape" frightened witness "Taylor" at Cave Run Marina, in Menifee County.[105]

Sightings continued into autumn 2006. Witness "Boyd" and his son saw a 7.5-foot creature, weighing 350 to 400 pounds, near Ashland in October. On November 5, a couple camped in Powell County's Red River Gorge awoke to growling sounds of a creature exploring their camp. They saw red eyes, noted a smell "like a ferret," then saw the beast flee "running on two feet, then four." One day later, three hunters near Martha (Lawrence County) heard wood-knocking sounds which they attributed to Bigfoot. On November 14, a Kenton County couple saw a hairy biped, four or five feet tall, walk past their rural home. Another autumn sighting, near Pineville, involved a shaggy biped seven to eight feet tall, with visible male genitalia. Witness "Josh" described the thing as "a very intelligent and humanlike creature with feelings and emotions, perhaps even thought." The year's last incident, on December 5, involved a report of heavy footsteps and weird growling in the foggy woods around a farm near Lawrenceburg, in Anderson County.[106]

The year 2007 produced six alleged Bigfoot encounters. At 4 a.m. on January 3, witness "Chris" detected a "rotten stench" and saw an apelike creature amble past his deer stand, near Cave City in Barren County. On January 23, two Boyd County residents heard a prowler outside their home, near Cattlesburg, and photographed a footprint that "was not [made by] any known animal." On March 28, Brad Law and his girlfriend were driving near Neboo (Hopkins County) when they met a dark-colored creature that walked on two legs but ran on all fours. One day later, a Simpson County farmer found a "large, white, hairy, clawed, and horned-type gorilla" sleeping in his backyard. When roused, it displayed "four large fangs" and retreated. The witness told GCBRO investigators, "We are seriously considering moving. This thing terrifies us every other night." On April 27, Montgomery County produced a report of biped closely resembling Simpson County's horned albino gorilla—except for its long, jet-black tail. Finally, on May 5, a Barren County hunter heard footsteps in the woods and smelled a foul odor, prior to sighting an eight-foot "hunched over" biped whose fingertips hung to its knees.[107]

The year 2008 produced nine specific Bigfoot sightings, one report of unexplained frightening sounds, and one vague claim of multiple sightings by anonymous witnesses. On January 27, witness Dana Puff was walking near her home in Danville, when she met an eight-foot biped covered in black hair, with "coal-black eyes." Members of an unnamed family claim multiple sightings of a large, foul-smelling creature between April and November 2008, but the location is unclear. The anonymous reporting witness claims to live near South Portsmouth, in Lewis County, but that town of 748 residents is actually located in Greenup County. Pam Lovins, a BFRO investigator from West Virginia, was drawn to the Daniel Boone National Forest in June 2008 by reports of a Bigfoot encounter near Cave Run Lake. She met the supposed witnesses on June 14 and accompanied them after nightfall to the scene of their alleged sighting. There, Lovins says, she captured an unknown bipedal creature on videotape, from a distance of fifteen to twenty feet. The creature's eyes reflected lamplight, but its face "in no way resembled what I had always imagined." The videotape remains under wraps at this writing. August 2008 brought three reports—of unidentified thrashing sounds in the woods near Russell (Greenup County) on the 10th; a sighting of an eight-foot, "really muscular" biped near Dover (Mason County) the 16th; and another sighting of a similar, "really built" beast near Augusta (Bracken County), on the 17th.[108]

38.
Daniel Boone National Forest. *Image Courtesy of U.S. Fish & Wildlife Service*

Autumn 2008 produced five more reports. The first, with no specific date, involved one of the same Clay County witnesses who claimed a sighting twenty years earlier. Alone this time, witness "Clay" described a slender beast that walked on two legs but ran on all fours. It had "the body of a dog with similar physical features," including a head that was "dog shape [sic] with long ears, and long nose gray as the body, but black around the mouth." October brought reports from Harlan, Washington, and Powell Counties. The first case involved off-road bikers who glimpsed a black bear near Evarts, then found four large humanoid footprints on an unpaved road. Four youths "snipe hunting" near Springfield, at 2:30 a.m. on October 17, glimpsed "a bipedal walking, human-like figure" in the forest. Four nights later, a couple camped near Slade were roused from sleep by "ear-piercing screams." Morning's light on October 22 revealed "strange tracks" nearby. Finally, on November 6, witness "Ryan" and his wife reported sounds "like a peacock screaming" from the woods around their home, near Alexandria.[109]

A Question of Identity

What are the hairy bipeds sighted in Kentucky for the past two centuries? Four basic theories presently address the subject, and while none has any proven application to Kentucky sightings, they deserve consideration here.

The first, hoaxes, includes both private pranks and journalistic fabrications. As revealed by author Chad Arment's archival research, certain Nineteenth-Century newspapers paid reporters to write "silly season" monster reports as entertainment for readers, and as a boost to flagging circulation. On the private front, hoaxers such as Ivan Marx, Rant Mullens, and Raymond Wallace faked Bigfoot tracks and films for decades, but their clumsy efforts deceived no serious researchers, and their activities were confined to the Pacific Northwest. Similar fakers may have operated in Kentucky, but if so, they have not been identified.[110]

Another explanation, outcast humans, applies primarily to Nineteenth Century "wildman" reports. Chad Arment suggests that "without a doubt, the vast majority of Wild Man reports found in early newspapers are men or women who found themselves outside of society, fending for survival in the wild"—but were they? That explanation may apply to wildmen of normal stature, particularly those seen wearing rudimentary clothing, but it cannot explain hairy giants seven to ten feet tall, with fangs and glowing eyes, leaving footprints fifteen to twenty inches long.[111]

The third and most common explanation for Bigfoot sightings, misidentification of known species, is a twofold response, involving both native species and "alien" exotics. Dismissing reports of unexplained sounds and odors, it is clearly possible for inexperienced, frightened people to mistake a large running animal—deer, bear, whatever—for something monstrous. Bears are most often suggested as Bigfoot suspects, since they may stand on two legs and approximate Bigfoot's stature. However, no bear native to Kentucky rivals the size of the larger bipeds reported, nor do their snouts resemble the flat, apelike faces generally described. Finally, while bears can waddle for short distances on their hind legs, none under any circumstances run or jump in that fashion, as Bigfoot nearly always does.[112]

Exotic species raise a different question, since (size aside) the apes of Africa and Asia bear a closer resemblance to Bigfoot. Even so, known apes move primarily by "knuckle-walking" on all fours, and all have feet resembling human hands, with an opposed big toe. The "giant wild chimpanzee" reported from New Jersey in 1926 proved, at its capture, to be a "modest little monkey" the size of a house cat, inflated by exaggeration—but how many stray exotics live wild in Kentucky or any other American state? Wildlife officials acknowledge breeding colonies of monkeys in

Florida, but no state admits to harboring gorillas, orangutans, or chim-panzees. Likewise, no zoo or private menagerie in Kentucky reports the escape of any large apes, either recently or in the past.[113]

The remaining theories—prehistoric survivors or species unknown to science—are equally unappetizing to skeptics. The former generally refers to Gigantopithecus, a huge ape presumed extinct for some 300,000 years, known today from fossil teeth and jawbones found in Asia since 1935. While no Gigantopithecus fossils have yet been discovered in the Western Hemisphere, some researchers speculate that the 10-foot, 1,200-pound primates may have crossed the Bering Strait land bridge with early humans migrating eastward from Asia. In size and general form, as reconstructed from its minimal remains, "Giganto" might well be a model for the Bigfoot/Yeti creatures reported from North America to the distant Himalayas of Nepal.[114]

Author Loren Coleman suggests two alternate theories for the ap-pearance of unknown primates in North America. He labels the first proposed unknowns "North American apes"—NAPES, for short—noting that the first recorded sighting of a "gorilla" in North America (near Gallipolis, Ohio, in 1869) predates coinage of the Bigfoot sobriquet by ninety-odd years. However, Coleman's NAPES produce distinctly apelike footprints, with sharply opposed big toes, which bear no resemblance to Bigfoot's oversized humanoid tracks. Meanwhile, Coleman and coauthor Patrick Huyghe dub the Pacific Northwest's classic Bigfoot an unknown species of "neo-giant," while subtly different "marked hominids" and "proto-pygmies" allegedly prowl the southern United States.[115]

As if this were not confusing enough, Coleman, Huyghe, and author Mark Hall posit the existence of yet another unknown primate species, collectively dubbed "devil monkeys." Ranging in height from four to six feet as adults, these creatures purportedly combine the snout of a baboon with a long bushy tail and peculiar three-toed feet, thereby ex-plaining aberrant tracks like those found in Clinton County, Kentucky, in 1973. Coleman further suggests that devil monkey sightings may explain some reports of kangaroos at large in North America, particu-larly those wherein supposed marsupials eat meat or otherwise behave in uncharacteristic ways.[116]

It should not be supposed that Coleman's theories have persuaded all—or even most—Bigfoot researchers in America. Ongoing, often acrimonious debate persists in print and through Internet newsgroups such as Coleman's Bigfoot group (Bigfoot@yahoogroups.com) and Forest Giants (ForestGiants@yahoogroups.com). Without proof of Bigfoot's existence, no resolution is possible.

39.
Artist's conception of a "devil monkey." *Artwork Courtesy of William Rebsamen*

6.

Stranger Yet

Kentucky reports of monsters and other strange creatures include many not confined to the broad categories covered in preceding chapters. This chapter examines some startling loose ends, presented chronologically from Kentucky's pioneer days to the Twentieth Century.

Giant Skeletons (1792-1965)

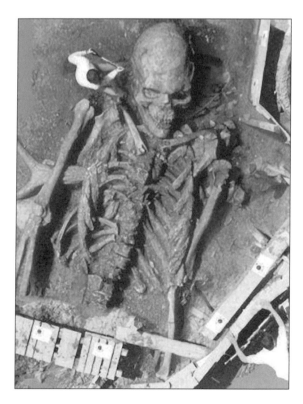

40.
Modern reports of giant skeletons often include hoaxed photographs. *Image Courtesy of Author's Collection*

Bluegrass historian Lewis Collins published his classic volume *Historical Sketches of Kentucky* in 1848. It includes the following description of giant human remains found by early settler John Payne at Augusta, near the Ohio River in Bracken County, during 1792. Payne wrote:

> The bottom on which Augusta is situated is a large burying ground of the ancients. A post hole cannot be dug without turning up human bones. They have been found in great numbers, and of all sizes, everywhere between the mouths of Bracken and Locust creeks, a distance of about a mile and a half. From the cellar under my dwelling, sixty by seventy feet, one hundred and ten skeletons were taken. I numbered them by the skulls; and there might have been many more, whose skulls had crumbled into dust....The skeletons were of all sizes, from seven feet to the infant. David Kilgour (who was a tall and very large man) passed by our village at the time I was excavating my cellar, and we took him down and applied a thigh bone to his—the owner, if well proportioned, must have been some ten or twelve inches taller than Kilgour, and the lower jawbone would slip over his, skin and all. Who were they? How came their bones there?[1]

Richard Collins updated his father's work in 1874 and republished it under the title *History of Kentucky*. That volume's timeline of Bluegrass history includes another case of giant bones, these found in Hardin County on August 15, 1850. According to that report: "The *Elizabethtown Register* records the finding, among the sands of Rolling Fork, twelve miles from that place, of the thigh bone of a human being, which measures in cubic inches six times the size of the thigh bone of a common man. A physician calculates the height of the giant of other days at 1twelve or thirteen feet."[2]

On January 5, 1858, the *Adair County News* reported yet another excavation of giant human bones from an "Indian mound" on Harrison Robinson's farm. Author George Eberhart, listing discoveries of giant human skeletons in his book, *Mysterious Creatures*, claims that similar finds have been made in Allen, Carroll, and Christian Counties, but he provides no further details.[3]

Kentucky's last published report of giant human remains came from Holly Creek, in Breathitt County, during 1965. Local resident Kenneth White was building cattle stalls adjacent to a stone formation, near his home, when he uncovered a "perfectly preserved skeleton" eight feet nine inches tall, with a skull that measured thirty inches in circumference. White showed the bones to folklorist Michael Henson, who later described them in his books *Tragedy at Devil's Hollow* (1984) and *More Kentucky Ghost Stories* (1996).[4]

According to Henson, "[T]he arms were extremely long and the hands were large. By comparison, the feet were very small." The massive skull's "eye and nose sockets were slits rather than cavities, and the area where the jaw bone hinges to the skull was solid bone. It would seem that the person could not have opened his mouth." How such a creature could survive, much less grow to giant adulthood, remains unexplained. Henson also claimed that another unnamed farmer had plowed up a sixty-pound stone axe and a twenty-inch flint blade, sometime in the 1940s. As for the giant skeleton, he says it was reburied, apparently without being photographed. Henson refused to pinpoint the location, and he took the secret to his grave in 1995.[5]

Unknown Canids (Nineteenth Century to 1978)

Harry Smith was born a slave in 1815 and spent his first half-century in bondage. At age seventy-six, he published a memoir titled *Fifty Years of Slavery in the United States of America*, which includes an account of his meeting with a huge unidentified creature. Smith provided no date, but placed the event along Dutchman Creek, which feeds the Salt River in Spencer County. While fishing at night with a friend, Tom Hardman, Smith heard a noise like distant thunder, accompanied by earth tremors that sent rocks tumbling into the creek. Looking downstream, both fishermen saw an animal eight feet long and four feet high at the shoulder. Smith compared it to a dog, while claiming that it had "no head or tail." The animal ignored them, passing on along the creek, where "nothing seemed to stop it in its course" until it vanished from sight. No evidence supports Bart Nunnelly's suggestion that the creature was "a possible Bigfoot walking on all fours."[6]

More than a century later, in spring 1978, an unknown "doglike animal, larger than a fox, with a long dark tail," attacked a pony at Prestonsburg, in Floyd County. *Fate* magazine reported the event in October 1979, saying that the horse was severely injured. The predator escaped and remains unidentified today.[7]

Goatmen (1840s-1970s)

Reports of fierce ogres, possessing the head and upper body of a human with the hoofed hindquarters of a goat, emerged from three Kentucky counties over a span of 130-odd years. Jan Thompson says that the first reports came from Livingston County, around Tiline, in the mid-1840s. Iron-ore miners in the area were prone to "mysterious" deaths, Thompson claims, sometimes accompanied by sightings of the Goatman. She elaborates to credit the monster with raids on livestock, and suggests (without any specific evidence) that the creature still makes annual appearances to "wreck havoc" on local farms.[8]

41.
"Goatmen" resemble legendary satyrs, like the one depicted on the right, in this Seventeenth Century painting. *Image Courtesy of Author's Collection*

A century after the first events in Tiline—if they ever occurred— another Goatman surfaced 156 miles to the east, along Pope Lick Creek in Jefferson County. Stories of the hybrid creature's origin vary, some describing it as an escaped circus freak, while others blame mingling of human and animal remains after a train plunged from the Norfolk

Southern Railway trestle spanning Pope Lick Creek, while enroute to a Louisville slaughterhouse. In any case, the beast was said to haunt that trestle through the 1940s and 1950s, luring hapless victims to leap from the bridge or throw themselves beneath the wheels of oncoming trains. Occasional fatalities from accidents or suicide perpetuated the legend, transforming the trestle and creek into prime sites for adolescent "legend-tripping." An eight-foot fence failed to deter trespassers, and director Ron Schildknecht paid homage to the creature in his 1988 film, *The Legend of the Pope Lick Monster.*[9]

Some legends are too colorful to die. Another Goatman visited Smith Mills, in Henderson County—115 miles west of Louisville, 51 miles east of Tiline—in the late 1970s. Bart Nunnelly interviewed one of the aging witnesses in 1993, recording a description of a true monstrosity with shoulder-length hair, short horns on its forehead, a hairy human torso, and split hooves of a "glowing yellow color" on its caprine hind legs. Nunnelly further notes that a Goatman was "possibly seen" in Spencer County, during January 2005. Despite the hooves and horns, he speculates that the Goatman may be "a Bigfoot with possible mange."[10]

Giant Birds (1866-2005)

42.
Bald eagles, like this one photographed at Lake Barkley, are Kentucky's largest known birds. *Image Courtesy of U.S. Fish & Wildlife Service*

Native American folklore is filled with tales of huge eagles, known collectively as "thunderbirds" and by a wide variety of other names in local tribal dialects. Kentucky's first published report of such a creature appeared in the *Atlanta Constitution* on September 18, 1866, lifted verbatim from a story in *The Democrat*, published in Cairo, Illinois. That item read:

> James Henry, of Mound City, Illinois, shot a new and comparatively unknown bird, on the Kentucky shore [of the Ohio River] opposite that city, which is thus described in the *Cairo Democrat*:

> It is larger than the ostrich, and weighs 104 pounds. The body of this wonderful bird is covered with snow white down and its head is of a fiery red. The wings, of deep black, measure 15 feet from tip to tip, and the bill, of a yellow color, 24 inches. Its legs are slender and sinewy, pea green in color, and measure 48 inches in length. One of the feet resembles that of a duck, and the other that of a turkey. Mr. Henry shot it at a distance of 100 yards, from the topmost branch of a dead tree, where it was perched, preying upon a full-sized sheep that it had carried from the ground. This strange species of bird, which is said to have existed extensively during the days of the mastodon, is almost entirely extinct—the last one having been seen in the State of New York in the year 1812. Potter has it on exhibition in his office at Mound City. Its flight across the town and river was witnessed by hundreds of citizens.[11]

In January 1870, Lincoln County's *Stanford Dispatch* described another unknown bird, considerably smaller than the Mound City specimen. James Pepples, residing two miles outside Stanford, allegedly met the bird on January 8, after local youths reported wild screams and sounds of clanking chains. According to the *Dispatch*:

> Mr. Pepples laughed at the alarm of the boys, but was still on the lookout for strange sights. On last Saturday his curiosity was somewhat relieved by seeing a monster bird, something like the condor of Sinbad the Sailor, alight on his barn. It gave a few of the screams which had so disturbed the boys, and Mr. P. was satisfied that he had found the ghost. He took down his rifle, and without precaution put in a silver bullet, drew a bead on the bird, and it fell. On approaching it he found that only one wing had been broken, which he amputated. Now comes the secret

of the chains. One foot had hanging to it a steel trap weighing about four pounds, which had been evidently set for varmint. It had been there for some time, as the flesh had rotted off, the trap only hanging by a leader. On measurement, the bird proved to be seven feet from tip to tip. It was of a black color, and both similar and dissimilar in many respects to an eagle. Its feet, and the feathers of its legs, which hung about six inches in length, were those of an eagle, but the jet black color indicated another species. At last accounts it was doing well, and eating raw flesh with a voracious appetite.[12]

The details of that story, ranging from the marksman's silver bullet to a wild bird "doing well" after it has been shot and had one wing hacked off, clearly suggests a hoax.

In 1950, two Lee County hunters reportedly fired at an unidentified bird with a twenty-foot wingspan. It escaped, despite their best efforts to kill it, and the incident was not reported until correspondent Michael Henson described the event in *Fate* magazine's August 1984 issue.[13]

43.
Some modern witnesses describe birds the size of small airplanes.
Artwork Courtesy of William Rebsamen

Multiple sources describe the next incident, wherein a postman at Maysville reported seeing a "giant birdlike creature in flight" on December 4, 1966. No further details are available, but the sighting occurred during the same period when a winged creature nicknamed "Mothman" was seen repeatedly around Point Pleasant, West Virginia. Furthermore, witnesses in Lowell, Ohio (138 miles from Maysville), saw four large birds—five feet tall at rest, with 10-foot wingspans—on November 26. Two days before the Maysville sighting, five pilots at an airport in Gallipolis, Ohio (eighty-three miles distant), reported a long-necked bird the size of a small aircraft, flying at seventy miles per hour.[14]

In 1970, a Johnson County hiker reported finding a large and "recently used" bird's nest atop a cliff at some unspecified location. The nest allegedly contained eighteen-inch feathers, but their disposition was not recorded.[15]

On May 16, 1977, four beagles—two adults and two pups—were playing outside Greg Schmidt's home at Rabbit Hash (rural Boone County), when a "very big, big bird" swooped down and snatched a five-pound pup, carried it for some 600 yards, then dropped it into a pond. A veterinarian in Walton, Dr. R.W. Bachmeyer, stitched the young dog's wounds and it recovered, while the bird escaped and remains unidentified. Four separate newspapers in Cincinnati and Lima, Ohio, covered the story—which came only two months before a pair of huge raptors tried to snatch ten-year-old Marlon Lowe from his yard in Lawndale, Illinois.[16]

Bart Nunnelly claims a personal giant-bird sighting at Smith Mills, in Henderson County, on April 11, 1998. Nunnelly was driving with his wife that Saturday, when they saw "a giant bird-like 'thing'" soar overhead. According to Nunnelly's published description, the creature had leathery skin, devoid of feathers, and sported no growth except fringes of "reddish-brown hair" on its legs. Its head "looked prehistoric," with a foot-long bony crest resembling that of a Late Cretaceous pteranodon, while its hindquarters sported a curled tail "with a short phalange on top." The animal's bare skin, says Nunnelly, was red and "wrinkly like an elephant's."[17]

Seven years later, in autumn 2005, a more conventional giant bird appeared to witness "E.D." and two companions in Bullitt County. Seen briefly in a farmer's field, first standing, then flying away, the bird had black feathers on its head and back, with a brown breast and belly. Compared to an adult Angus bull in the same field, it stood five feet tall at rest, and had a wingspan of fourteen to sixteen feet. With wings spread, E.D. claimed, it was "easily twice the size of the bull."[18]

Flying Humanoids (1880+)

On July 28, 1880—nineteen years before the Wright brothers built their first box kite in the rough form of a biplane—Louisville residents Ben Flexner and C.A. Youngman saw a strange object in the sky overhead. At first, they took it for a balloon, but as it drew closer they beheld "a man surrounded by machinery which he seemed to be working with his hands." Flapping fins or wings protruded from the flier's back, propelling him through the air and controlling his altitude by moving at various speeds until he vanished from sight in the lowering dusk.[19]

A century later, a rather different winged humanoid appeared near Golden Pond, outside Cadiz in Trigg County. Self-styled paranormal investigator Jan Thompson relayed the tale from unnamed third parties, providing no dates but claiming that the event occurred "about three years ago." Thompson's witnesses, two elderly women, were traveling by car when they saw a "demon from Hell" standing in the middle of the road. It was seven feet tall and nude, with grayish-green skin like ostrich hide, pointed ears, a "pencil-thin mouth," and glowing red eyes "the size of eggs." When their car had closed to a range of twenty feet from the creature, it spread leathery wings and flew away, swooping low over the vehicle in passing. Thompson claims two other sightings of an entity that looked "about the same," one from Grand Rivers (Livingston County) in the 1920s, and the other from Trigg County in the mid-1970s.[20]

Hopkins County's "Varmint" (1951-52)

This still-unidentified creature appeared for the first time in early November 1951, clawing trees at the home of George Eades on U.S. Highway 62. Days later, on November 14, Mrs. Elvis Fugate heard her dog "go wild" at 10:30 p.m. and saw a "big black animal" walking along her driveway, "snorting like a horse." She frightened it away with pistol fire, but it did not go far. A motorist on Highway 12 soon reported a large black beast with a bushy tail, crossing the road in front of his car. By December 27, when Madisonville's *Messenger* published its first "varmint" report, there were seven incidents on file. Farmer Roy Hunt of Menser logged four beastly visits, including clawed trees and large, unidentifiable footprints. Members of his family described the animal's nocturnal calls as a "low whistling sound, like the sound made by someone blowing in a gun barrel."[21]

Matters went from bad to worse in January 1952, as the prowler turned predator. Lawrence Peine saw the hulking beast behind his home at Wayside Grove, on January 4, and found a pig carcass the next day, hanging from a claw-scarred tree. On January 7, residents of Dawson Springs reported hearing sounds of "several dogs in a large battle." The next morning, Everett Ausenbaugh found bloodstains and "varmint" tracks in the forest. On January 13, a group of 100 hunters scoured the woods around Menser and Charleston, but found no trace of their quarry. Meanwhile, at 11:15 that morning, Isaac Parker glimpsed a "timber wolf" crossing a rural lane between Ilsley and Carbondale. Five hours later, witness Bernie Ausenbach saw a similar beast in the same area.[22]

45.
Lake Peewee, outside Madison, in the "varmint's" domain.
Image Courtesy of U.S. Fish & Wildlife Service

Undeterred by hunters, the varmint left more tracks around Ilsley on January 19, then slaughtered a sixty-pound hog on Herbert Gambling's farm, in the nearby Southard community. Orvill Lantaff saw the creature south of Earlington on January 24, and mail carrier J.W. Nisbett logged a sighting near Madisonville on January 25.[23]

Bloodshed resumed on February 2, when Gus Hunt found a pig mutilated and partially eaten on his farm, north of Manitou. The following day, two of W.H. Hickman's hunting dogs suffered wounds in a fight with some unseen assailant, on Brown Road. Something invaded Otis Tippett's rabbit hutch on February 4, breaking the necks of two twenty-pound rabbits and gnawing one carcass. W.H. Hickman found four of his pigs mauled to death on February 7. Two days later, the varmint entered a hog lot in Madisonville, ducking gunshots from Johnny McRoy. On February 10-11, an estimated 300 hunters turned out with 15 hounds and an aerial spotter, but they went home empty-handed.[24]

Madisonville policeman J.B. Bard and a friend, Edgar Arnold Jr., tried a different tactic the following week, strewing fresh meat and bones along Brown Road as bait. Two nights in a row, some prowler snatched the meat and fled, unseen. On February 17, Bard and Arnold saw "a large dark animal" approach their trap, but it turned and fled when they stepped from their car. Arnold fired a shotgun blast at the retreating form, but missed it cleanly from 100 yards. Nothing remained but footprints, which measured 4.5 inches by 3.5 inches when cast in plaster. While larger than a dog's paw prints, the tracks were deemed "much smaller" than the varmint's.[25]

On February 23, 1952, locals gathered at Henry Whitfield's feed store to organize the Varmint Hunters Association of Madisonville and Hopkins County. They elected J.B. Bard as president, with Whitfield's wife as secretary and one Jim Stewart as treasurer. VHA by-laws required each member in good standing to "openly admit that you believe there is a Varmint in Hopkins County," to spend at least three hours daily in pursuit of same, and to pay one dollar toward a reward for the hunter who killed or captured the beast. President Bard set an example for his members by leaving the first meeting early, to launch a new hunt, but it was all in vain. The varmint made its last appearance on April 4, dodging shots fired by Jeddie Faver of Barnsley.[26]

The varmint was not without its detractors. Robert Towe, editor of the *Hopkins County Times*, led the critical assault, blaming varmint sightings on "a long sought, gnawing hunger for additional industry in Hopkins County." To support his view, Towe consulted Brady McClain, an agent with the Department of Fish and Wildlife Resources, who opined that claw marks found on local trees had been inflicted by a prankster with a pitchfork. McClain believed that W.H. Hickman's dogs were mauled by a raccoon, but he offered no opinion as to what had killed no less than seven hogs and two rabbits between January 5 and February 7. Towe's campaign of ridicule climaxed on March 11, with publication of a long poem titled "The Varmint Speaks," by Sara Brown of Madisonville. Towe hailed the facetious poem as revealing "a heretofore unknown accomplishment of the Varmint. He speaks."[27]

Whatever the varmint was or was not, it remained a local topic of debate for decades. Speculation that it may have been a gray wolf (*Canis lupus*), including a report that one Isiah Burden killed a wolf near Anton in 1919, contradicts official listings of both the gray wolf and red wolf (*C. rufus*) as extirpated from the state.[28]

"Dogmen" and "Werewolves" (1951-2006)

Throughout America, eyewitnesses report encounters with hairy bipedal creatures whose protruding, fanged snouts, and aggressive demeanor break the classic Bigfoot mold. Author Linda Godfrey has catalogued modern reports of these "dogmen" or "werewolves" across the Midwest and Northeast in two excellent books: *The Beast of Bray Road* (2003) and *Hunting the American Werewolf* (2006) But at last report her files included no Kentucky cases. For accounts of Bluegrass dogmen, we must once again rely on Bart Nunnelly and perennial witness Jan Thompson.

46.
Werewolf legends
pervade human history.
*Image Courtesy of Author's
Collection*

While neighboring Indiana boasts werewolf tales dating from the Eighteenth Century, alleged wolfmen were slow to cross the Ohio River. The first story recounted by Nunnelly dates from 1951 and was related by his own mother. As a ten-year-old living in Henderson, she and several of her relatives sighted a bipedal creature that "looked like a large dog in the face," but was "hideously disfigured with what looked like numerous terribly deep scars." A quarter-century later, in 1975, witness "Jennie W." saw a six-foot shaggy biped with a dog's snout and "long, sharp-looking teeth" beside Boyd County's Route 168, between Ashland and Catlettsburg. Boyd County also produced four Bigfoot sightings between 1991 and 2007, but none of those creatures had a pointed nose to match the thing seen in 1975.[29]

Ashland's creature resurfaced in the 1980s, frequenting a local cemetery where it was reported leaping ten-foot gates. Nunnelly refers to multiple unnamed witnesses, including one who saw the "evil-looking thing with a wolf head and fangs" on two separate occasions. In one instance, two policemen sent to explore the graveyard allegedly fled after glimpsing the beast. Various witnesses reported that it ran with equal speed on two legs and all four. Regrettably, the coverage of that monster "flap" omits any substantive details needed to investigate the claims.[30]

We examined Jan Thompson's alleged Bigfoot sightings in Chapter 5, but the vicious, dog-faced "Beast of LBL" that menaced her at Grand Rivers in 1978 sounds more like a dogman, from its snout and fangs to its "mournful wolf's howl." She subsequently told Bart Nunnelly that the creature was "kind of a cross between the werewolf and Bigfoot," adding her tale of an early 1980s tourist massacre committed by the monster and covered up by stunned police. That story proved impossible to verify by press time for this book[31]

Nunnelly's next dogman report dates from autumn 1991, when ex-forester "Chris" and a friend met one of the beasts near Cynthiana, in Harrison County. They were driving on an unpaved forest road when a three-foot-tall biped resembling "a slightly shaggy monkey with lupine legs" darted through the beams of their headlights. Based on his experience with woodland fauna, Chris insisted that the thing did not belong to any known species.[32]

Kentucky dogman sightings continue in the Twenty-first Century. Greenup County logged an incident "a few years" before 2007, when "a big 'werewolf-looking' thing completely covered with shaggy hair" leaped over a motorist's moving vehicle. In spring 2001, witness "Mark M." reported unearthly howling around a friend's Trigg County home, but did not see the beast responsible until June 2006, when he glimpsed a pair of large amber eyes watching him in the forest, from a point eight feet above the ground. Their placement "implied" that the creature had a canine muzzle, but it remained invisible.[33]

Kelly's Goblins (1955)

While alleged "flying saucers" and alien "close encounters" fall outside the purview of this volume, one famous case often cited in UFO literature deserves inclusion here. Many accounts describe the strange events as taking place at Hopkinsville, in Christian County, but they actually occurred at Kelly (population 150), seven miles farther north.[34]

On August 21, 1955, eleven persons gathered at the home of Glennie Lankford, fifty-year-old widowed matriarch of the Lankford-Sutton clan. Also present were her children, Lonnie, Charlton, and Mary; adult sons Elmer and John Sutton, from a previous marriage, with their respective wives Vera and Alene; Alene's brother, O.P. Baker; and two visitors from Pennsylvania, Billy Ray Taylor and his wife, June. The Taylors, like Elmer and Vera Sutton, were part-time traveling carnival workers.[35]

Around 7 p.m., Billy Taylor left the house to draw water from an out-side pump. He ran back seconds later, describing an "immense shining object" that had fallen from the sky, descending toward a gully located a quarter-mile from Glennie Lankford's home. The others present laughed and ignored his report, prompting future students of the case to suggest that Taylor "had a low standing" within the Lankford-Sutton clan.[36]

Roughly an hour after Taylor's "flying saucer" sighting, the family dog began barking excitedly. Taylor and Elmer Sutton stepped outside and saw a bipedal creature three or four feet tall walking toward the house. It had "large eyes, a long thin mouth, large ears, thin short legs, and hands ending in claws." Rushing back into the house, Sutton grabbed a shotgun, while Taylor seized a .22-caliber rifle. Both men fired on the strange creature at close range, whereupon it performed a back-flip and fled into the woods, seemingly unscathed.[37]

Thus began a chaotic three-hour ordeal, in which multiple elfin creatures terrorized the besieged family, peering through windows, scaling the cabin's roof, and clambering into nearby trees. One snatched at Billy Taylor's hair, as he passed beneath its leafy perch. The creatures seemed impervious to gunfire, one "floating" to the ground when it was blasted from a tree. Despite promiscuous discharge of firearms, none of the weird visitors was visibly injured. None left a drop of blood at the scene. At last, the human combatants piled into two cars and raced off to Sheriff Russell Greenwell's office in Hopkinsville.[38]

Greenwell initially thought they were joking, then reluctantly agreed to visit the "battle" site. Upon arrival, Greenwell and his deputies found no trace of the creatures, but confirmed numerous bullet holes in the cabin's walls and windows. Twenty-plus officers scoured the vicinity and came back empty-handed, aside from statements by neighbors who confirmed "lights in the sky" and sounds of gunfire from the Lankford home. Greenwell stated that none of the witnesses were intoxicated, and all seemed genuinely frightened.[39]

After the police departed, the creatures allegedly returned for an-other skirmish, prompting more gunfire from the besieged cabin occu-pants. The next morning, Sheriff Greenwell called the U.S. Air Force, resulting in a military search and serial interrogations that produced no new evidence. Billy Taylor and Elmer Sutton left the scene before Air

Force officers arrived, while four other members of the clan—June Taylor and the three Lankford children—claimed they saw nothing, all being "too frightened to look" throughout the protracted encounters.[40]

Various mundane explanations were advanced for the Kelly events. Sheriff Greenwell denied that any of the witnesses were drunk, but in 2005 retired state trooper R.N. Ferguson told author Joe Nickell that he thought the Kelly creatures "came in a container" of alcohol. A neighbor also remarked on finding "a few beer cans in a rubbish basket" at the Lankford home, the day after the incidents. An alternative theory, that the witnesses were tormented by monkeys that escaped from some unnamed zoo or circus, fails to explain descriptions of the creatures and their seemingly bulletproof hides.[41]

The "Bedford Creature" (1962/1975)

Irish author Ronan Coghlan, writing in 2004, tells us that Bedford's unknown entity of 1962 was "a creature that walked on its hind legs and seemed to have features like a dog, puma, or bear, but was not identical with any of those creatures." Furthermore, "Its arms reached its knees and it had black hair." Thirteen years later, Coghlan adds, "several creatures which made noises like pigs were heard (and perhaps vaguely seen) in a nearby wood along the banks of the Ohio. There was also some evidence of unknown creatures in cornfields."[42] Inquiries conducted for this book failed to elicit any additional details.

Lizard Men (1966-75)

Reptilian creatures of humanoid form are a staple of UFO sightings, but various examples have been seen throughout North America sans "flying saucers." One such appeared to a witness known only as "Joseph" at Stephensport (Breckenridge County), in early autumn 1966.[43]

Joseph was nine years old when the incident occurred, but four decades elapsed before he reported it to Bart Nunnelly in September 2006. As he recalled the event, a sound of something moving outside his house woke him at 1 a.m. and he rushed to his window, beholding a bipedal "lizard man" in the yard. It was "very amphibious looking," stood approximately six feet tall, and had a "hard-looking face" with small eyes, "similar to a snake or lizard." A "ridge-like feature" sprouted from the creature's forehead, running back over the crown of its head, and "kind of peaked at the top." Upon noticing Joseph, the thing turned and fled, running on its hind legs toward Sinking Creek, a tributary of the Ohio

River located 75 yards from Joseph's home. Bart Nunnelly interviewed Joseph and states that he "appeared very credible."[44]

47.
Reports of "lizardmen" defy rational explanation.
Artwork Courtesy of William Rebsamen

Nunnelly reports another lizard man encounter nine years later, in October 1975, from Milford, in Trimble County. We examined the July 1975 appearance of Milford's "giant lizard" in Chapter 3, together with garbled accounts by authors who misplaced those events in October, but Nunnelly adds a new twist to the tale. Specifically, while granting that witness Clarence Cable reported seeing a fifteen-foot reptilian quadruped, Nunnelly offers that unnamed "other witnesses" described the beast "as looking like a giant lizard that walked upright and was tailless."[45]

Nunnelly further suggests that Tennessee's captive "wild man," allegedly displayed in Louisville, Kentucky, during autumn 1878, may have been a reptilian creature. Most researchers treat that creature as a specimen of Bigfoot, though the *Courier Journal* of October 24, 1878, described its skin as "covered with a layer of scales, which drop off at regular periods, in the spring and fall, like the skin of a rattlesnake." We may rightly question how reporters knew what the thing's skin did in spring, and it apparently vanished sometime in November. Aside from scales, it also had "hair on his head and a dark reddish beard about six inches long." The eyes, far from small and reptilian, were "at least twice the size of the average-sized eye." A subsequent report of the creature, published in California on February 1, 1879, described it as "a man fish" with webbed fingers and toes.[46]

"Gravediggers" (1970-2001)

As with so many other Kentucky monsters, we owe our minimal knowledge of these strange creatures to Bart Nunnelly. During 2006, he collected reports from three witnesses—identified as "Terry" (or "T.W."), "Billy," and "A"—who saw the creatures in different counties, spanning three decades.

Terry's sighting occurred in spring 1970, while he and a friend were fishing near Shelby City, in Boyle County. Required to be at home by noon, Terry was walking back alone when a four-foot-tall creature leaped onto the railroad tracks in front of him, thirty to forty feet distant. Its fat body was covered with "real fine fur," surmounted by a round head which rotated like an owl's. Its face resembled a bat's, down to its pointed and "almost transparent" teeth. It stood upright, though Terry never saw its legs, and had hairless "spindly" arms, whose hands displayed clawed fingers and thumbs. Glimpsing Terry, it fled "like a blur" toward a nearby cemetery marked by gaping "huge holes" in the ground. Terry's grandmother heard his story and dubbed the creature a "gravedigger," suggesting that it excavates corpses.[47]

Twenty years later and 126 miles farther east, witness Billy saw a similar creature near Dorton (Pike County) in June 1990. His first glimpse of the beast suggested "a very large white dog," but as Billy drew closer, he saw that the thing stood "on two legs hunched over with small arms very high on its body." In general form, it resembled a kangaroo, and Billy thought that if it stood fully erect it might be seven feet tall. Billy subsequently claimed "gravedigger" sightings by various other locals, including a personal friend who saw the "white beast" perched in a tree, but details are sparse. Like Terry's sighting, Billy's occurred near railroad tracks and an old rural graveyard. Billy photographed a "possible" paw print left by the creature, resembling that of a large dog.[48]

A similar creature appeared briefly to witness "A" and three Martin County companions in 2001. The four were hunting raccoons after sundown, when their truck bogged down in mud. While they were struggling to free it, their headlights illuminated a creature described by "A" as a bipedal "kangaroo-bodied dog" with long brown fur and a "hunched over" posture. Its eyes were yellow, and its canine snout bristled with three-inch-long teeth. Bart Nunnelly logged "A's" report in December 2006 but reached no conclusions concerning the creature's identity.[49]

The "Sturgis Vampire" (1983)

We briefly examined this story from Jan Thompson in Chapter 5, but it deserves further consideration here. Jan relates a "guardian tale" on her Internet website about this creature. The supposed event occurred in the predawn hours of Christmas Day 1983, while Thompson was driving home from Indiana, traveling on country roads between Sturgis and Morganfield. In the midst of a snowstorm, a nude male figure ran into the glare of Thompson's headlights and paused, staring at her vehicle.[50]

As described by Thompson, the thing was nearly human, more than six feet tall, with milky-white skin over most of its body. Its red-eyed face, however, featured flat nostrils and was otherwise purely bestial, with a bloody fanged muzzle and tangled hair hanging below its shoulders. Ragged claws tipped the fingers of its abnormally long, slender hands. Before the creature fled, Thompson had time to note its penis, "uncircumcised and strangely hefty for a human."[51]

Upon reaching home, Thompson heard stories of local livestock mutilations performed by some unseen nocturnal prowler. She kept her sighting secret, fearing ridicule, but later overcame that reticence to publish it with other tales of her meetings with creatures unknown to science.[52]

Dwarf Apes (1990-1998)

Shortly before midnight on July 4, 1990, fourteen-year-old Christopher Walker and four friends were idling near a factory on the outskirts of Henderson, when they noticed movement from a nearby wooden crate. Suddenly, a stunted figure waddled into view on short bowed legs. It was covered with dark hair of uniform length, yet had "a mangy look about it." Red eyes glared from a simian face, surmounted by visible ears "like a pig's." After a ten-second face-off, the boys bolted and ran back to Walker's house, a half-mile distant from the factory. Adults, when apprised of the sighting, dismissed it as fantasy.[53]

A year later, Walker heard a similar tale from another friend, not involved in the July 4 incident. That unnamed witness had been crossing Henderson's Washington Street Bridge when he heard sounds like screams from a woman in pain. Seconds later, a small hairy "thing" emerged from the bridge's shadow, running on two legs toward a nearby drainage tunnel. It paused briefly to face the witness, revealing its red eyes and pointed ears, then screamed once more and vanished underground.[54]

When interviewed by Bart Nunnelly in 2006, Walker added a strange twist to his original story, claiming that the apelike creature had been wearing threadbare, tattered clothing. That claim seems to contradict Walker's original description of a creature covered "head-to-toe" by hair.[55]

Nunnelly's certainty around this case derives, at least in part, from an experience reported in 1995 by his brother and two youths identified only as "Tim S. and Chris W." At the time, Robert Nunnelly lived on a farm near Summer Shade in Metcalfe County. When chickens began disappearing, Robert and his friends mounted a stakeout. After nightfall, they saw "a considerable group" of "little hairy creatures" two or three feet tall, which chattered and grunted like apes. Caught in a spotlight's beam, some of the prowlers ran on two legs, while others dropped to all fours.[56]

A few nights later, Robert and the boys went hunting for the simian creatures, joined by Chris W.'s father. They surprised another covey of the "weird little boogers," noting that this batch was plastered with mud. Furthermore, the beasts' forelegs "looked somewhat longer than the back ones," a condition which did not prevent them from running "straight up a tree without slowing down at all."[57]

A final sighting of the diminutive creatures occurred in May 1998, with Robert Nunnelly's son and a friend as witnesses. On that occasion, they saw a larger apelike creature, four or five feet tall, chasing a cow across the farm's pasture. The creature abandoned the hunt and fled after blundering into a barbed-wire fence. It left strange footprints described as resembling a human's, "except for the toes, which appeared to be split-footed."[58]

Little People (1990-2005)

Global mythology is rife with tales of pygmy races, often magically empowered, that interact with human beings for good or ill. Early Cherokee tribesmen, inhabiting the region from North Carolina through Tennessee and Kentucky, believed that the tiny cave-dwelling nunnehi ("stone men") revealed themselves to humans as a forecast of impending disaster.[59] And while such tales are easily dismissed as fantasy, sightings of Bluegrass "little people" have continued into modern times.

48.
"Little people," like these alleged English fairies photographed in 1910, are reported from every continent. *Image Courtesy of Author's Collection*

In 1990, Donald Patton was a fourteen-year-old resident of eastern Kentucky, self-described as "absolutely obsessed with throwing rocks." He spent every free moment honing his skills in the woods near his home—for which, sadly, he gives no specific location. One evening, while he was lobbing stones at trees, Patton's father appeared and summoned him home. As Donald started back toward the house, Mr. Patton called into the woods for Donald's brother Eric and a family friend named Matt. When Donald told his father that he was alone, Mr. Patton said he had seen two small figures standing behind Donald as he approached. Donald's response, that he had gone into the woods alone, prompted an armed search of the property, during which Mr. Patton again saw, then lost, two figures roughly four feet tall and dressed all in white, like "a damn doctor or something." The experience frightened both father and son, but the stunted prowlers did not reappear.[60]

Seven years later, in autumn 1997, witness Sharon Rogers saw an elfin figure less than three feet tall, dressed in brown-and-tan garb that included a cape and peaked cap, standing across the street from her Glasgow home in Barren County. Rogers published her tale in the June 1998 issue of *Fate* magazine and subsequently sat for an interview with author Bart Nunnelly. To this day, she insists that the figure she observed was not a child in costume, but rather "an adult with normal proportions in accordance with its height." Its long hair and outfit seemed to be "plucked straight out of the Middle Ages," resembling classic sketches of woodland fairies.[61]

On June 24, 2003, witness "Steve W." embarked on a canoe voyage along western Kentucky's Rough River. Stopping at the Falls of Rough, in Breckenridge County, he was overcome by an inexplicable "queasy, nervous feeling" and "sensed death." Later that day, and several miles downstream, he camped and found a clay pot partly buried on the river's bank, its lid impressed with "little hand marks." He assumed that they were paw prints from a curious raccoon, but as he pried off the pot's lid, Steve heard a sound "like little kids laughing" nearby. A further search revealed two pale-skinned figures roughly ten inches tall, dressed in leather pants with suspenders and matching peaked caps. Both had red hair and blue eyes. Though seemingly aware of Steve's presence, they persisted in their task of dragging a tree stump through the woods, with aid of leather thongs, until Steve heard "a loud snap" and they vanished, along with the stump and clay pot.[62]

In December 2006, Bart Nunnelly interviewed an unnamed witness from Hebbardsville (Henderson County) whose personal sightings included both Bigfoot encounters and two surprise meetings with little people whom the witness called "Joui-stee." As described to Nunnelly, the Joui-stee were mischievous "spirit entities" who favored green clothing with pointed hats and moccasins, passing their leisure time with music and dancing. Based on personal observation, the witness opined that the Joui-stee resembled Irish leprechauns and served as "spiritual helpers of the pure at heart," living in harmony with Bigfoot near ancient Cherokee burial sites.[63]

Bart Nunnelly's endorsement of those tales as truthful stems, at least in part, from his own reported discovery of tiny hand-made artifacts during his childhood in Henderson County. His first "pygmy flint" was a supposed leather punch, barely one-quarter of an inch in length. Years later, Nunnelly found a quartz arrowhead smaller than his pinky fingernail, "executed so exquisitely" that he concluded it must be the work of tiny tools and craftsman's hands. His published work does not explain what happened to those artifacts.[64]

Hyenas at Large (2004-2005)

On the afternoon of December 4, 2004, Emily Edwards and her husband were driving on Interstate 64 near Lexington, when they observed a car parked on the highway's shoulder with its emergency flashers blinking. Slowing on their approach, they saw a strange creature standing some ten feet in front of the vehicle. It resembled a hyena with "bluish-gray" fur and dark spots, a "fringe" of fur along its spine, and sloping hindquarters. As they passed, it snarled and bared wicked-looking fangs. Mrs. Edwards later estimated that the beast stood three feet tall at the shoulder.[65]

49.
Kentucky witnesses report encounters with creatures resembling Old World hyenas.
Image Courtesy of U.S. National Oceanic and Atmospheric Administration

Twenty months later and 184 miles to the west, construction worker James Berry had a similar encounter on Highway 318, near Uniontown. Berry was driving home from work at 5 p.m. when he saw a creature the size of a fawn "cavorting" in a roadside field. A closer look revealed a canine head and ears, a brown coat with black patches, and hind legs significantly shorter than the forelegs. Berry later told Bart Nunnelly that the creature, seen clearly in daylight from 60 feet away, could only have been a hyena.[66]

That said, the four known species of hyaenids, including three hyenas and the aardwolf, are indigenous to Africa and Asia.[67] Any seen roaming around the Bluegrass State would be dismissed as fugitives from some menagerie.

Unless ....

Another hyena-like creature, known to Native American tribesmen as shunka warak'in ("carrying-off dogs"), has been reported from various sectors of the United States and Canada for over a century. One specimen was shot and killed by Montana farmer Israel Hutchins in 1886. It measured forty-eight inches long from snout to rump (tail excluded) and stood twenty-eight inches tall at the shoulder, with sloping hindquarters and "an odd-shaped head." Hutchins traded the carcass to taxidermist Joseph Sherwood for a cow, whereupon Sherwood stuffed and displayed it in his storefront "museum" at Henry's Lake, Idaho. Upon Sherwood's death, the specimen passed to Idaho's Museum of Natural History, where it was "lost" for decades. Curators found it in storage, in November 2007, and returned it to a descendant of Hutchins, but he declined requests for DNA testing. Concerning the strange beast's identity, he rhetorically asked journalists, "Do we want to know?"[68]

The mystery remains unsolved.

Pine Hill Phantoms (2005-2006)

Bart Nunnelly's next report of an unknown creature comes from "the Pine Hill area" in Rowan County. Perhaps he means Pine Hill Cemetery, since the town of Pine Hill stands seventy-odd miles to the southwest, in Rockcastle County.[69] In any case, the area produced two strange sightings within a span of seventeen months which deserve inclusion here.

The first incident, involving several unnamed witnesses, occurred on the evening of June 1, 2005. Nunnelly reports that a "strange animal" was seen descending from a tree and running off into the woods. Observers said that it was "bigger than a cat, but smaller than a cougar"—or, as Nunnelly suggests, "about the size of a dog." The only other detail offered is a reference to "spikes" running along the creature's spine.

That feature calls to mind the chupacabra ("goat sucker," in Spanish), a vampiric predator first reported from Puerto Rico, later seen as far afield as Argentina, Spain, and the American Southwest. However, in the absence of the chupacabra's trademark livestock raids, the comparison is imprecise.[70]

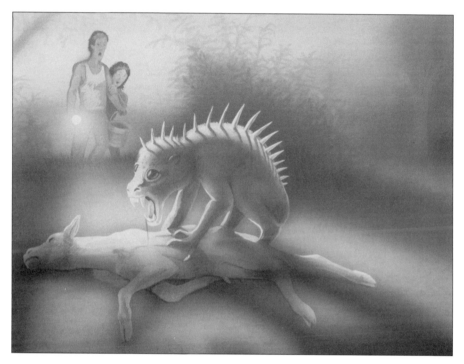

50.
A beast seen at Pine Hill Cemetery in 2005 resembled Puerto Rico's chupacabra.
Artwork Courtesy of William Rebsamen

November 2006 brought a different report from the district, this time involving "a giant owl that gave off a yellow glow." Nunnelly also alludes to UFO sightings in the same neighborhood, but no further details are available. Curiously, reports of hauntings also emanate from two other Pine Hill Cemeteries, in Hollis, New Hampshire, and Westfield, Massachusetts.[71]

Conclusion
Where Next?

Nearly 200 years have passed since Georges Cuvier declared that no new species of any significant size awaited discovery on Earth. When he spoke those hasty words in 1812, science recognized only 5,738 animal species. By 2000 the list had grown to 1.8 million species, with no end in sight.[1] A random sampling of recent zoological discoveries includes the following:

* June 2002: Dutch scientist Marc Van Roosmalen discovered two unknown species of monkey in Brazil's Amazon jungle, ranked as the thirty-seventh and thirty-eighth new primate species found since 1990. Thirteen of those new species were discovered in Brazil alone.[2]

* June 2003: A team led by Dr. Michael Harvey, a tropical biologist from Florida International University, announced the discovery of seven new species from the Bolivian Andes. Their finds included two frog species, two snakes, two toads, and one lizard. The team also documented the existence of a known owl species never previously found within Bolivia.[3]

* April 2005: Researchers in Madagascar discovered two new species of lemur, bringing the total number of recognized species to forty-nine. Edward Louis, a conservation geneticist from Omaha's Henry Doorly Zoo who made the discovery, told journalists, "I think we'll top a hundred [species] in five years." During the same month, biologists from the Nature Conservation Foundation discovered a new monkey species in India.[4]

* September 2006: Dr. Enrico Bernard and his team of researchers from Conservation International reported their discovery of forty previously unknown species of animals and

plants in Brazil's Amapá region. Those discoveries prompted Brazilian lawmakers to protect the "lost world" by creating the Amapá State Forest.[5]

* June 2007: Leaders of an expedition sponsored by Conservation International announced discovery of twenty-four new species on remote plateaus in eastern Suriname, located eighty miles from the nation's capital.[6]

* September 2007: Spokesmen for the World Wildlife Fund reported the discovery of twenty-one new species from the "Green Corridor" of Vietnam's Annamite Range, east of the Mekong River. The same region yielded several new, large quadrupeds in the 1990s.[7]

* October 2007: Marc van Roosmalen's team of researchers identified a new species of peccary in Brazil. That find brought the total of van Roosmalen's discoveries to twelve new species, including four marmosets, two monkeys, a dwarf porcupine, a dwarf manatee, a dwarf tapir, a brocket deer, and a new species of Brazil nut.[8]

* April 2008: Conservation International announced the discovery of fourteen new animal species from the Brazilian rain forest, noting that their habitat is already threatened by unfettered logging.[9]

* September 2008: Julian Caley, a biologist from the Australian Institute of Marine Science, announced the discovery of 130 new coral species, 100 new isopod crustaceans, and other previously unknown creatures along the Great Barrier Reef. "People have been working at these places for a long time," Caley said, "and still there are literally hundreds and hundreds of new species that no one has ever collected or described."[10]

Kentucky, of course, is not a "Third World" nation covered by trackless rain forests. In 2006, the state's population stood at 4,206,074 year-round inhabitants, amounting to 101.7 persons per square mile, occupying 1,888,164 housing units. Kentucky's three national parks logged 275,581,547 visitors—ninety percent of the total U.S. population—in 2007 alone.[11] Surely no beasts of any size could hide in such a crowded state.

Or, could they?

Bear Essentials

Consider the case of the American black bear (*Ursus americanus*), found in abundance by early Anglo-European settlers in Kentucky. By 1850, hunting and habitat destruction allegedly had extirpated the species statewide. Authors Roger Barbour and Wayne Davis could not document a single living specimen within the Bluegrass State in 1974.[12]

Case closed? Not quite. Black bear sightings from Bell, Fleming, Harlan and Powell Counties persisted through the 1940s, but were generally dismissed as hoaxes or cases of mistaken identity. Then, in 2003, Dr. David Maehr, professor of wildlife and conservation biology at the University of Kentucky, documented a "small breeding population" of black bears in the Cumberland Mountains, which encompass Bell and Harlan Counties. His explanation—that bears had "returned" to Kentucky from neighboring states—ignored the possibility that some may have lingered despite their supposed extirpation.[13]

51.
Black bears, once nearly extirpated in Kentucky, are now plentiful.
Image Courtesy of U.S. Fish & Wildlife Service

State authorities initially considered the rediscovery of black bears a "good sign" for Kentucky, a testament to official progress in restoring the environment, but that soon changed. Complaints from rural residents prompted a statewide legal ban on feeding bears, enacted during 2002 and buttressed with warnings from the Department of Fish and Wildlife Resources. Terry Brock was fined $250 in 2004, for killing a bear in his backyard at Mayking (Letcher County), but DFWR spokesmen changed their tune four years later, asking lawmakers to approve a "limited hunting season" on bears.[14]

Adult black bears may be seven feet tall when standing on their hind legs. The largest specimen on record weighed 881 pounds.[15] They are so large, in fact, that skeptics commonly attribute Bigfoot sightings to glimpses of bears in the wild. That raises further questions in Kentucky, where black bears were presumed to be as mythical as Bigfoot between 1850 and the latter 1990s. We are thus compelled to ask: If bears somehow avoided being noticed in Kentucky for 150 years—or sightings were officially dismissed as false—what else may yet be found within the Bluegrass State?

Aquatic Mysteries

Kentucky is a relatively dry state—only 1.7 percent of its land lies underwater, versus eight percent for neighboring Ohio—but it still offers ample sanctuary for aquatic species. Kentucky is the only U.S. state bordered on three sides by rivers, including the Mississippi to the west, the Ohio to the north, and the Big Sandy and Tug Fork to the east. Within the state itself, 11,212 rivers and streams course over 90,000 miles, while 416 lakes and reservoirs cover 696 square miles.[16]

As for swamps, while Kentucky claims only fifteen identified by name, those wetlands shelter diverse species and may not have yielded all their secrets yet. Marshall County boasts five separate swamps, with the largest—Cypress Creek Swamp—sprawling over 284 acres. Ballard County's only wetland, Axe Lake Swamp, is half again that size, drowning 458 acres.

52.
Cypress Creek Swamp, in Madison County. *Image Courtesy of U.S. Fish & Wildlife Service*

Henderson County has two swamps, while other counties claiming one apiece include Butler, Carlisle, Christian, Hopkins, Livingston, Simpson and Union.[17]

It may be mere coincidence that eight of those ten counties contribute fourteen percent of Kentucky's recorded Bigfoot sightings. Henderson County alone logs a dozen, while Christian and Hopkins claim three each; Livingston, Simpson and Union list two each; and Ballard and Marshal have one apiece.[18] Should Bluegrass Bigfoot hunters focus their primary attention on Henderson County's Grassy Pond Slough and Little Swan Pond Slough?

53. Do Kentucky's swamps conceal unknown creatures? *Artwork Courtesy of William Rebsamen*

Whether unknown primates gravitate toward swamps or not, Kentucky's lakes and waterways have produced enough eyewitness sightings of unknown creatures to warrant further exploration. Herrington Lake is the deepest in Kentucky, at 249 feet, and three counties—Boyle, Mercer, and Garrard—share its 2,335-acre expanse. If we accept the story told by Profesor Lawrence Thomas in 1972, it may harbor more than known species of striped, white, and yellow bass.[19]

The Ohio River comprises 665 miles of Kentucky's northern border, from Catlettsburg to its mouth, where it empties into the Mississippi. Kentucky thus abuts sixty-eight percent of the Ohio's 981-mile length and feeds it with numerous tributaries, any of which may grant access to inland waterways. In 1999, Onis Davis hooked the Kentucky's record catfish (104 pounds) on the Ohio, near Cannelton Dam.[20] The Ohio River's reported aberrant life forms include Bart Nunnelly's giant turtle, the serpentine beast known as "Genny," and two errant cephalopods. Even if the latter are attributed to hoaxers, it does not explain the first such report, logged from a major Ohio River tributary.

That feeder, the Licking River, stretches over 320 miles, draining much of northeastern Kentucky between the watersheds of the Kentucky River to the west and the Big Sandy River to the east. Ecologists deem the Licking River a unique ecosystem for its region, with its lower reaches ranked as a rare native muskie stream. Other Licking River fish found nowhere else in Kentucky include blue suckers, eastern sands, mimic shiners, paddlefish, redside dace, slender madtoms and streamlined chubs. The river also supports fifty species of mussels, eleven of which are endangered. The state's record common carp (fofty-four pounds fourteen ounces) was pulled from the Licking's South Fork by fisherman Ricky Vance in 1971. Thirteen years later, Brian and Pat Mulloy caught a flathead catfish weighing 79.5 pounds near Boston.[21] Still, the Licking River's strangest catch remains the octopus found there in 1959.

Another Ohio River tributary, the Green River, rises in Lincoln County and flows over 300 miles to reach its terminus at Covington. Record fish from the Green River include Esker Carroll's flathead catfish (ninety-seven pounds) in 1956; Larry Caldwell's freshwater drum (thirty pounds) in 1980; Norman Moran's bowfin (fourteen pounds eight ounces) in 1999; Howard Hilliard's blue sucker (four pounds fifteen ounces) in 2001; and Donny Johnson's bighead carp (fifty-two pounds), also in 2001.[22] While impressive in their own right, none rival the serpentine creatures seen by Brad Nunnelly in 1998.

What else resides in Kentucky waters? The discovery of an outlawed snakehead in 2005, though found in private hands, raises the possibility of other specimens at large. More worrisome yet are the reports of piranhas pulled from the Ohio River. Kayla Shuits caught a thirteen-inch specimen in August 2001, while Terry Schneider and John Turkovich hooked a twelve-incher in early September. Their catch was billed as "the third in a month," but no details of the second fish were forthcoming. Kyle Owens caught an apparent piranha in June 2007, and while exotic fish dealers dismissed it sight-unseen as a related (but harmless) pacu, no arguments were raised concerning the red-bellied piranha landed by George Palmer in August 2007. No verified piranhas have yet been pulled from Kentucky waters, but pacus have been found in Lake Cumberland (1991) and in Trigg County (1993).[23]

55.
Harmless pacus like this one are often mistaken for piranhas. *Image Courtesy of U.S. Fish & Wildlife Service*

54.
Ferocious piranhas feature in legends and Hollywood films. (A NEW WORLD PICTURE RELEASE) *Image Courtesy of Author's Collection*

Woodland Wonders

Proceeding from the water to dry land, we find that forty-seven percent of Kentucky is covered by forests, 11.9 million acres in all (down from 25 million acres when the first Anglo-European settlers arrived). While eighty-nine percent of Kentucky woodlands are privately owned, the federal government controls 852,508 acres comprising the Daniel Boone National Forest, the Cumberland Gap National Historical Park, and the Big South Fork National River and Recreation Area. Nine state forests cover 39,388 to 43,158 acres, according to contradictory official sources. Altogether, Kentucky has one of the most diverse hardwood species mixes in the nation.[24]

Wherever would-be monster hunters live in Kentucky, woodlands are within their reach. The Daniel Boone National Forest's 707,000 acres include parts of sixteen counties, including Bath, Estill, Jackson, Laurel, Lee, McCreary, Menifee, Morgan, Owsley, Powell, Pulaski, Rockcastle, Rowan, Wayne, Whitley and Wolfe. Big South Fork National River and Recreation Area spans the Kentucky-Tennessee border, with one-third of its 125,310 acres lying in McCreary County. Cumberland Gap National Historical Park includes 20,508 acres in Bell and Harlan Counties. Kentucky's state forests, in descending order of size, include: Pennyrile State Forest, comprising 15,468 acres of Christian County; Kentucky Ridge State Forest, with 15,251 acres in Bell County; Dewey Lake State Forest, covering 7,353 acres of Floyd County; Kentenia State Forest, spanning 4,277 acres in Harlan County; Knobs State Forest and Wildlife Management Area, with 1,539 acres in Bullitt County; Marrowbone State Forest and Wildlife Management Area, including 1,125 acres in Cumberland and Metcalfe Counties; Green River State Forest, with 1,106 acres in Henderson County; Tygarts State Forest, covering 874 acres in Carter County; and Olympia State Forest, with 800 acres in Bath County.[25]

Where Be Monsters?

Would-be monster hunters in Kentucky may improve their odds, at least in theory, by seeking unknown creatures where they appear most frequently. To that end, we complete our Bluegrass survey with a ranking of specific counties, based upon the number of "monster" sightings reported from each. The cases sited here are detailed in preceding chapters and in the appendix, which includes a definitive list of Bluegrass Bigfoot reports.

Seven counties stand out at once, as centers of monstrous activity.

Western Kentucky takes the honors for multiple reports, with four counties in the top six. Researcher R.D. Norris claims "dozens" of black panther sightings from neighboring Livingston and Marshall Counties; Livingston also leads with two Bigfoot reports and a goatman sighting, against Marshall's lone account of an unidentified primate. Henderson County, nearby, claims twelve Bigfoot sightings, two black panthers, two encounters with dwarf apes, a giant bird, a dogman, and a report of elfin creatures. Trigg County, farther to the southwest, has seven Bigfoot sightings on record, plus encounters with a dogman and a flying humanoid. Jefferson County, in north-central Kentucky, boasts seven Bigfoot reports, two black panther sightings, and single reports of a cougar, a goatman, and an airborne human. Casey County, near the state's heart, has ten Bigfoot sightings on file.

Counties with seven monster reports on record include the following: Boyd, with five Bigfoot reports and two dogman sightings (which may represent the same creatures); Daviess, with six Bigfoot sightings and a giant snake; Harlan, claiming five Bigfoot encounters, one black panther, and a giant snake; Lawrence, with seven Bigfoot reports; Martin, with six Bigfoot sightings and one "gravedigger" report; and Union, including five Bigfoot reports, a hyena at large, and Jan Thompson's "Sturgis vampire."

Three counties report six monster sightings each. Residents of Boone claim five Bigfoot encounters and one meeting with a giant bird. Reports from Calloway County include three Bigfoot sightings, two cougars at large, and one giant snake. Henry County divides its sightings between three Bigfoots and three "extinct" cougars.

Three more counties list five monster sightings apiece. Crittenden County has logged four Bigfoot reports and one panther sighting. Mason County ties Crittenden on Bigfoot sightings and adds a giant bird. Spencer County is more diverse, with three Bigfoot reports, an unknown canid, and a giant snake.

A dozen Kentucky counties list four monster sightings on their resumes. Barren County logs two Bigfoot reports, one incident involving little people, and one giant snake. Campbell County claims two Bigfoot sightings, one cougar report, and one case of an unidentified big cat. Christian County balances three Bigfoot cases with one little-men encounter. Clinton County's three Bigfoot reports are balanced with a panther sighting. Hopkins County's "varmint" of 1951-52 shares the record book with three Bigfoot reports. Johnson and Lincoln Counties tie with three Bigfoot sightings and one giant bird report each. Kenton County residents report three Bigfoot encounters and a cougar at large. McCreary nearly duplicates that record, with three Bigfoot sightings and one black panther report. In Oldham, fruitless searches for a cougar and a giant snake are balanced by the captures of a reed cat and a serval. Lewis and Perry Counties each claim four Bigfoot sightings.

Ten Bluegrass counties claim three creatures each. In Breathitt, Bigfoot reigns supreme with three sightings. Breckenridge is more diverse, with one sighting each of Bigfoot, little people, and a lizard man. Six counties—Greenup, Logan, Lyon, Madison, Pike and Rockcastle—each claim two Bigfoot sightings; they complete their respective tallies with dogmen (Greenup and Lyon), a tiger (Logan), a cougar (Madison), a "gravedigger" (Pike), and Pine Hill Cemetery's phantoms (Rockcastle). Metcalfe and Trimble Counties are unique in claiming no clear-cut Bigfoot reports. Metcalfe makes do with three dwarf-ape sightings, while Trimble offers a giant lizard, the Bedford Creature, and the elusive Pope Lick Monster.

Ten counties with two reports each complete our survey of regions with multiple monster sightings. Grayson and Letcher Counties each claim one Bigfoot encounter and one cougar on the prowl. Morgan, Taylor and Russell Counties likewise balance lone Bigfoot sightings with black panther reports. Harrison County logs a Bigfoot sighting and a dogman report, while Lee County matches Bigfoot against a giant bird. Three other dual-monster counties claim no Bigfoot sightings: Bullitt reports a cougar and a giant bird; Fayette claims a giant snake and a hyena; while Floyd logs a cougar and a mystery canid.

In Search Of ....

It is axiomatic that "monster" sightings cannot be predicted—unless, of course, they are hoaxed. Sighting "flaps" such as those involving the Pope Lick Monster and Hopkins County's varmint end as suddenly and enigmatically as they begin, with or without recovery of such supporting evidence as footprints, mutilated animals, or damaged property. No honest would-be monster hunter can expect a sighting, and any frequency of incidents reported by any one person adds fuel to the fire for skeptics. They are quick to question credibility.

Whether or not that view is fair, pursuers of unclassified creatures must plan on being held to an exacting standard. Mere eyewitness testimony, while preferred above all else in courts of law, is virtually worthless in the scientific field, at least where sightings of a new and unknown creature are concerned. Regardless of a given witness's credentials—be they scientific specialists, police, clergy, or trusted public figures—they face contradiction, even outright ridicule, from skeptics and professional debunkers who insist that such things cannot be.

In terms of circumstantial evidence, standards of proof are likewise elevated far beyond the legal standard. Photographs or videotapes of a crime in progress may convict defendants, even condemn them to death, but the same evidence will not satisfy skeptics that new and unusual creatures exist. Photographic evidence can be—and has been—faked in various high-profile cases involving Bigfoot, lake monsters, and so-called "sea serpents." Heated controversy still surrounds the brief film clip of a supposed Bigfoot shot by Roger Patterson in October 1967. While qualified experts—including the late Dr. Grover Krantz, professor of physical anthropology at Washington State University, and Dr. Jeff Meldrum, a specialist in vertebrate locomotion at Idaho State University—have analyzed that film and pronounced it authentic, critics (some of whom refuse to even view the film) reject the possibility of any unknown primates still at large. Somewhat incredibly, one critic of the film has identified two separate individuals as Patterson's alleged "man in the monkey suit."[26]

Footprints, again, may prove a case in court, but when reported as the spoor of an "extinct" or unknown creature, the same arguments apply. Veteran trackers squabble over supposed cougar paw prints, with die-hard skeptics attributing even the largest prints to dogs. The matter of footprints is central to Bigfoot research, but hoaxers such as California's Raymond Wallace undermine serious study. When Wallace died in 2002, his relatives claimed that he had "invented Bigfoot." Despite the fact that unknown biped sightings across North America predate Wallace's birth by more than a century, credulous reporters (including Dan Rather at *CBS News*) repeated that fiction as fact. Meanwhile, forensic scientists confirm that certain casts of Bigfoot tracks display realistic dermal ridges and/or apparent deformities never found in hoaxed footprints. Thus far, no such casts have been made in Kentucky, but 1997 produced one from Pike County, Georgia.[27]

Other physical evidence has proved problematic. In 1926, Scottish embryologist John Graham Kerr published a peer-reviewed article describing a curious fossil found in the Gran Chaco region of South America. He claimed it was a 2.5-inch viper's fang, belonging to a monstrous prehistoric snake that Kerr dubbed Bothrodon pridii. Thirteen years later, the relic was identified as a prong from the shell of a Chiragra spider conch (*Lambis chiragra*). More recently, DNA testing of hairs and feces collected from the scenes of hairy-biped sightings in Asia and North America has yielded intriguing results, indicating that the samples came from unclassified primates, but the donors remain unidentified.[28]

In Kentucky, while supposed Bigfoot hairs have been collected on at least five occasions, none have been scientifically tested. Three of those samples—from Trimble County in 1962, Henderson County in 1975, and Fleming County in 1980—were found (and presumably discarded) before Sir Alec Jeffreys pioneered DNA profiling at Britain's University of Leicester, in 1984. Two Lawrence County residents found stool with clinging hairs at the scene of a 1992 Bigfoot sighting, but they did not collect samples. Witness Joanna Carter preserved "long and nappy" hairs from the site of a 2000 sighting in Harlan County, but she has refused to submit them for testing, which prompts accusations of hoaxing.[29]

Author and publisher Chad Arment suggests a four-step process for researching anomalous creatures. The steps include recognition, information gathering, collection of evidence, and—ideally—identification.[30] When pursued in a systematic fashion, the steps occur as follows:

Recognition of a subject is the critical first step, and should not be confused with identification. While countless articles and books describe pursuit of "unknown" animals, simple logic rules out any such behavior. Literally unknown creatures cannot be pursued, since no one recognizes their existence. New, undreamed-of species are only discovered by chance, as when the first megamouth shark (*Megachasma pelagios*) became entangled in a ship's anchor chain, in 1976. As of July 2008, another forty specimens had been obtained, but none were known before the holotype was snagged by accident. Conscious pursuit of any animal demands prior indications that it may exist, whether those indications derive from folklore, published accounts, or word-of-mouth eyewitness reports.[31]

From recognition that a creature presently unrecognized by science (or officially deemed nonexistent within a particular region) may exist, the would-be tracker should proceed with **information gathering** before a physical attempt is made to locate specimens at large. Archival research normally includes perusing media reports and any published articles or books that may contribute useful knowledge of the animal's alleged appearance, its behavior, and its habitat. In some cases—Bigfoot, the Loch Ness Monster, etc.—the literature may be extensive; for more obscure creatures, sources may be limited to brief newspaper articles or local folklore. Researchers should be critical in their assessment of media reports, particularly with regard to Nineteenth Century newspaper articles that were sometimes hoaxed as "silly season" filler.[32]

A useful tactic, where feasible, is personal correspondence or interviews with witnesses identified in media reports or otherwise. Such debriefings may provide details ignored in previous reports and/or correct misinformation spread through media accounts or rumors. Personal contact with witnesses should help researchers evaluate their claims, and if a witness is deemed credible, specific questions may enhance the would-be monster hunter's quest. Critical information may include the specific location, time of day, and season when sightings occur; weather conditions and other surrounding circumstances; topographical details of the sighting location; plus specific details of the animal's appearance and behavior that may be omitted or misreported in second and thirdhand accounts. Interviewing techniques, refined through experience, should permit researchers to determine if a witness seems credible or is prone to exaggeration, if his story changes over time, if he craves publicity, and if his story is influenced by prior reports of the creature in question.[33]

Aside from re-examination of museum or laboratory specimens, which may identify "new" species, **collecting evidence** of an unrecognized creature's existence will involve field work. That effort need not be a full-dress safari to some exotic location. Indeed, particularly with regard to some of the hypothetical Bluegrass fauna discussed in Chapter 1, it may be a literal walk in the park, but any systematic effort deserves at least some rudimentary planning.

Practicality comes first. Round-trip logistics for a monster hunt include provisions for transportation, clothing, and other gear (dictated by terrain and climate), compliance with legal requirements (permits, licenses, restrictions imposed on specific activities or weapons), even preparation for emergencies (first-aid or snakebite kits, reliable means of communication). Wildlife photography demands a different set of skills and gear than making plaster casts of footprints. The consequences of misjudging terrain or mishandling equipment may range from simple frustration to crippling injury or death.[34]

In terms of evidence desired, photographs and/or videotape are the least persuasive to skeptics, for reasons already discussed. Casts of suspect tracks are better, but production of clear, detailed casts may require advance practice. Better still is some organic remnant of the animal itself—blood, feathers, feces, hair, even the cast-off skin of a reptile—which may be subjected to DNA testing by wildlife genetics experts if the hunter's budget permits it. The best evidence, of course, is a complete specimen, living or dead, which may become the holotype of a new species or confirm survival of a creature thought to be extinct.[35]

Clearly, the difficulty of obtaining specimens depends upon the rarity, ferocity, and size of the creature in question. In broad terms, hunting techniques are either active or passive. Active methods, as described by naturalist Ivan Sanderson, include stalking, running-down (high-speed pursuit on foot or in a vehicle), and driving (as where teams of beaters chase prey toward a waiting hunter). Only the first technique seems practical for Bluegrass cryptozoologists, since the animals they seek rarely display predictable behavior. Passive methods involve use of traps, poison, or bait that lures a creature to some point where it may be captured or killed. All may be circumscribed by law, and even if conducted with the full approval of authorities may end unhappily. Poison and traps are indiscriminate, and even "honest" mistakes have consequences.

Kentucky law does not permit hunting of cougars—protected by federal law, although presumed nonexistent within the state's borders—or other big cats. Likewise, while there is no hunting season on Bigfoot or "thunderbirds," careless hunters who mistakenly shoot black bears or eagles invite prosecution.[36]

Even without conclusive evidence, researchers may collect enough data to sketch profiles of their quarry. That process, which Chad Arment dubs "biological modeling," involves educated guesswork rather than manipulating evidence to support preconceived notions. Just as eyewitness descriptions of vertically-undulating spines demonstrate that most reported "sea serpents" cannot be reptiles, evidence collected in pursuit of local mystery beasts may confound expectations and contradict so-called "conventional wisdom."[37]

Formal **Identification** and description of a new or rediscovered species must rely on credentialed experts. Detailed physiological examination of specimens, including their genetic markers, falls outside the skill set of most amateur hunters, who may mistake cases of aberrant coloration, sexual dimorphism, or genetic mutation for an undiscovered species. Furthermore, the process of publishing descriptions in peer-reviewed scientific journals and assigning two-part scientific names in Latin is generally closed to random members of the public at large. With that in mind, researchers who succeed in collecting specimens should contact recognized authorities in the respective field, rather than calling press conferences and offering their finds for sale to the highest bidder.[38]

That said, no one, regardless of his or her station in life, is debarred from the pursuit or chance discovery of anomalous fauna. Amateurs often lead the way, particularly in pursuit of creatures that mainstream science refuses to consider. At worst, the quest may represent an engaging hobby; at best, a step toward academic immortality.

Enjoy the hunt.

Appendix
Bigfoot in Kentucky

The following timeline presents abbreviated information on all alleged Bigfoot encounters reported from Kentucky from the Eighteenth Century through early 2009. Undated incidents appear at the end of the list.

Abbreviated sources include:

BFCU: Bord and Bord, Bigfoot Case Book Updated
BFE: Bigfoot Encounters website
BFRO: Bigfoot Field Researchers Organization
COTE: Coleman and Clark, Creatures of the Outer Edge
GCBRO: Gulf Coast Bigfoot Research Organization
IBS: International Bigfoot Society
KBF: Kentucky Bigfoot website
OBSG: Ohio Bigfoot Search Group
STAAU: Green, Sasquatch: The Apes Among Us
THB: Arment, The Historical Bigfoot
UX20: Bord and Bord, Unexplained Mysteries of the Twentieth Century

Date:	1770s?
Witness:	Daniel Boone
Location:	Unknown
Report:	Boone claimed to have killed a ten-foot hairy "Yahoo."
Source:	IBS #2697

Date:	1870s
Witnesses:	Harold Holland and others unnamed
Location:	Allen County
Report:	Settlers report a population of apelike creatures living in a wooded valley called "Monkey Cave Hollow." Harold Holland claims to have seen the last "monkey," killed by a hunter "80 years or thereabouts" before Holland described the beast to Ivan Sanderson (who died in February 1973).
Source:	STAAU, p. 222

Date:	October 1878
Witnesses:	Various unnamed

Location:	Louisville, Jefferson County
Report:	Showmen display a "wild man of the woods" caught in Tennessee. It stands six-foot- five inches tall and is covered with hair or scales, according to different reports.
Sources:	BFCU, p. 220; THB, pp. 304-6; Louisville *Courier-Journal*, Oct. 24, 1878

Date:	August 1892
Witnesses:	Dr. H.W. Dimmit and others
Location:	Vanceberg, Lewis County
Report:	A hairy "wild man" of "gigantic stature" hurls stones at local residents.
Source:	THB, p. 161

Date:	May or November 1894
Witnesses:	Joseph Ewalt, Joe Smith, Eph Boston and sons
Location:	Washington County
Report:	Farmers track a six-foot-five-foot chicken-stealing "hairy monster" to its cave, then flee with out confronting it. Ewalt says the creature wore a sheepskin as a loincloth.
Source:	BFCU, pp. 22, 221; THB, pp. 161-3

Date:	March 1907
Witness:	Jim Peters
Location:	Buena Vista, Garrard County
Report:	Farmer sees a hairy figure wearing "a coonskin tied around its loins," chasing a dog. Trackers find humanoid footprints but cannot locate the "escaped lunatic."
Source:	THB, pp. 163-4

Date:	1920s
Witnesses:	Jerry LaGrange, Ed Laven, Res Shoemaker
Location:	Perry County
Report:	Trappers hear nocturnal sounds "like a female screaming" and "think it was a Bigfoot."
Source:	IBS #2829

Date:	1930s
Witnesses:	Charlie Nickell and family
Location:	Haldeman, Rowan County
Report:	Large apelike creature attempts to enter a rural home, then flees armed pursuers, leaving "giant sized footprints."
Source:	Jewell Castle correspondence, August 2007

Date:	April 1944
Witness:	Ellis Elkins
Location:	Paintsville, Johnson County
Report:	Tall hairy creature with a bushy tail attacks a fisherman on the Big Sandy River and steals his fish.
Source:	IBS #170

Date:	1940s and 1950s
Witnesses:	Various unnamed
Location:	Pope Lick Creek, Jefferson County
Report:	Multiple witnesses claim sightings of the "Pope Lick Monster," sometimes confused with Kentucky's "Goat Man."
Source:	GCBRO

Date:	1950
Witness:	Unnamed
Location:	Boone County

Report:	Researcher John Daily cites unspecified news clippings on the appearance of a Bigfoot nicknamed "Satan."
Source:	*Creature Chronicles* No. 2

Date:	1950 "approximately"
Witnesses:	"Joe" and friends
Location:	Martin County
Report:	Teenage campers see a bipedal figure seven to eight feet tall, with glowing red eyes.
Source:	BFE

Date:	Summer 1950
Witnesses:	Unnamed children
Location:	Beauty, Martin County
Report:	Children playing along the Tug River meet a six-foot hairy biped carrying a large stick in one hand.
Source:	BFRO #5678

Date:	1951
Witnesses:	Three unnamed
Location:	Near Wolfpen Hollow, Johnson County
Report:	Witnesses see a creature nine to ten feet tall prowling outside their rural home at night.
Source:	BFRO #2155

Date:	October or December 1953
Witnesses:	Two unnamed
Location:	Liberty, Casey County
Report:	Children see a hairy primate using a stick to dig up dirt behind a neighbor's house. They flee as it approaches, baring "large" teeth.
Sources:	BFRO #1024; GCBRO; KBF

Date:	1956 or 1957
Witness:	Two unnamed
Location:	Pilgrim, Martin County
Report:	Baptist minister and his wife see a shaggy biped watching their house from 75 to 150 feet away.
Source:	BFE; KBF

Date:	1957
Witnesses:	"Phyllis" and two relatives
Location:	White Ash Hill, Lee County
Report:	"Something large and frightening" blocks passage of a rural road, running back and forth across the pavement and lobbing holly branches for twenty to thirty minutes, until nocturnal travelers retreat.
Source:	KBF

Date:	May 15, 1957
Witness:	Unnamed
Location:	Wilson Ridge, Casey County
Report:	A five-year-old child panics after seeing a "hairy man" in his back yard in mid-afternoon.
Sources:	GCBRO; KBF

Date:	Late 1950s
Witnesses:	Two unnamed
Location:	Cary, Bell County
Report:	Teenagers exploring abandoned coal mines see a "gray or white looking ape type animal on two legs," approximately eight to nine feet tall.

Source:	BFRO #2364; KBF.

Date:	February 1959
Witness:	Unnamed
Location:	Covington, Kenton County
Report:	A motorist's report of Bigfoot standing on a highway bridge coincides with sightings from nearby Cincinnati.
Sources:	BFCU, p. 234; STAAU, p. 209

Date:	1960
Witnesses:	Three unnamed
Location:	Casey County
Report:	Bigfoot enters a barn where three girls are playing.
Source:	GCBRO

Date:	1960
Witness:	Unnamed
Location:	Casey County
Report:	Drive-in movie owner sees an apelike creature while taking his projectionist home after work.
Source:	GCBRO

Date:	1960s
Witness:	Unnamed
Location:	Grove Ridge, Casey County
Report:	Large hairy "varmint" frightens a coon hunter's dogs, which henceforth flee each time they encounter its scent.
Source:	GCBRO; KBF

Date:	1960s
Witness:	Unnamed
Location:	U.S. Highway 127, Casey County
Report:	Teenage girl sees an apelike creature peering through her second-story bedroom window.
Source:	GCBRO; KBF

Date:	June 1962
Witnesses:	Owen Pike (or Powell) and others
Location:	Trimble County
Report:	Residents report dogs and livestock slaughtered. One describes a black six-foot biped attacking his dogs, while others see a beast "not quite a dog, a panther, or a bear." Claw marks and black hairs found at a barn where calves were killed remain unidentified.
Sources:	BFCU, pp. 73-4; STAAU, p. 223

Date:	July 1962
Witnesses:	Four unnamed
Location:	Near Mount Vernon, Rockcastle County
Report:	Two couples parked on "lover's lane" see a growling man-sized creature "hopping" toward their car "hunched up on all fours."
Source:	BFCU, p. 74; KBF

Date: 1964	
Witnesses:	four unnamed
Location:	Near Butler, Pendleton County
Report:	Young bicyclists see a hairy biped resembling a gorilla "but much larger" emerge from the cellar of an abandoned house.
Source:	KBF

Date:	July 1964
Witnesses:	Several unnamed
Location:	U.S. Highway 36, Grant County

Report:	Sightings of a Bigfoot with "shiny eyes" at a local garbage dump spark chaotic monster hunts that leave two teens wounded by reckless gunfire.
Source:	KBF

Date:	1965
Witness:	Unnamed
Location:	Goose Creek, Casey County
Report:	Retired state trooper hears a nocturnal "yowler" in the woods.
Source:	GCBRO; KBF

Date:	1966 or 1967
Witness:	Unnamed
Location:	Brownies Creek, Bell County
Report:	Man walking home between 2 and 3 a.m. sees "something extremely tall, hairy, and big" with glowing red eyes. Locals call the site "Bugger Mountain." The man's mother claims a sighting at the same place, a few days later.
Sources:	BE; KBF

Date:	1968
Witnesses:	Dr. Richard Young and Charles Denton
Location:	Murray, Calloway County
Report:	Nocturnal travelers see a hairy primate cross the road.
Sources:	BFCU, p. 252; STAAU, p. 253

Date:	Late 1960s
Witness:	Unnamed
Location:	Near Jabez, Russell County
Report:	Driver on Highway 196 sees a "large ape creature" cross the road.
Source:	KBF

Date:	1968
Witness:	Unnamed
Location:	Reed, Henderson County
Report:	Motorist sees a large hairy biped cross Collins Road.
Source:	KBF

Date:	October 1969
Witness:	Unnamed
Location:	Livingston County
Report:	Motorist sees a four-foot biped covered in "dull white" hair cross a rural road, twenty-five feet in front of his car.
Sources:	GCBRO; KBF

Dates:	Late 1960s to early 1970s
Witness:	"M.F."
Location:	Hebbardsville, Henderson County
Report:	Witness claims "countless sightings by dozens of different individuals," spanning several years. Bipedal creatures eight to twelve feet tall frequently steal and kill livestock.
Source:	KBF

Date:	"197?"
Witness:	James Vincent
Location:	Black Hollow, Cumberland County
Report:	Hunter tracks a foul-smelling biped that left fifteen-inch footprints. The hunt is "apparently unsuccessful," but locals recognize the creature(s) as "Wild Woolly Bullies."
Source:	KBF

Date:	"197?"
Witness:	Unnamed
Location:	Vanceburg Hill, Lewis County
Report:	School bus driver sees a "big man" covered with reddish-brown hair, with a "caveman" face, emerge from woods and cross the road.
Source:	BFRO #6210

Date:	1971
Witnesses:	Several unnamed
Location:	Reed, Henderson County
Report:	Bart Nunnelly reports Bigfoot "very active" but few specifics are available. Residents of Carlinsburg Road see a large biped with "glowing green eyes," while a motorist on Collins Road reports a nocturnal sighting.
Source:	KBF

Date:	Summer 1971
Witnesses:	"Patrick" and his mother
Location:	Pleasure Ridge Park, Jefferson County
Report:	Residents hear nocturnal howling from the woods around their home on several occasions.
Sources:	BFRO #2385; IBS #634 and 2984

Date:	October 1972
Witness:	Unnamed
Location:	West of Russellville, Logan County
Report:	Deer hunter reports a moonlight encounter with Bigfoot. He describes a biped 7 to 8 feet tall, weighing 500 pounds, seen from a distance of 20 to 30 feet.
Sources:	BFRO #2390; KBF

Date:	Summer 1973
Witness:	Three unnamed
Location:	Near Berea, Madison County
Report:	Teenage campers see a creature 7 to 8 feet tall walking through the woods at 2 a.m.
Source:	BFRO #2428

Date:	Autumn 1973
Witnesses:	Charlie Stern and others unnamed
Location:	Albany, Clinton County
Report:	Residents report "many" sightings of a Bigfoot "family" including two adult primates and a "youngster." Farmers blame the creatures for killing livestock. Charlie Stern fires close-range gunshots at a 6-foot black creature with a bushy tail and an "ape/human face," but it escapes, leaving 3-toed footprints.
Sources:	BFCU, p. 274; COTE, pp. 114-16; KBF

Date:	1974
Witnesses:	Two unnamed
Location:	"Rattling Bridge Road," Calloway County
Report:	While driving on a country lane at dusk, witnesses see a hairy biped 6 to 7 feet tall cross the road 150 feet ahead of their car.
Source:	GCBRO

Date:	September 1974
Witness:	Unnamed
Location:	Broughtentown, Lincoln County
Report:	Girl walking dogs in the woods sees a "huge, long-haired wide thing" from 15 to 20 feet. Her father finds three large footprints.

She and relatives subsequently hear "sounds of trees crashing and loud noises" on various occasions.

Source: GCBRO

Date: 1975
Witness: Unnamed
Location: Hamlin, Calloway County
Report: "Large hairy Bigfoot seen." No further details available.
Source: KBF

Date: 1975
Witnesses: Unnamed
Location: Spottsville, Henderson County
Report: Various residents along Mound Ridge Road, near the Green River, report Bigfoot encounters by day and night. Police allegedly confiscate evidence including footprint casts and hair samples after livestock mutilations. A "reliable witness" claims Bigfoot communicates telepathically with "supernatural powers."
Sources: BFCU, p. 284; STAAU, p. 223; KBF

Date: Summer 1975 or 1976
Witness: "John D." and friend
Location: Pritchett Farm, Henderson County
Report: Motorcyclists observe an unknown biped from 100 to 150 yards, described as 7 to 8 feet tall, weighing 350 pounds.
Source: KBF

Date: August 9, "1975-77"
Witness: Unnamed
Location: Nolin Lake Estates, Grayson County
Report: While camping, child sees a large gray-haired "man thing." He somehow recalls the precise date, but not the year.
Source: BFRO #10765

Date: September 15, 1975
Witness: Unnamed
Location: Breathitt County
Report: Witness sees an eight-foot biped outside his rural home and goes outside, where he is "overcome by a horrible smell" and finds a large pile of feces in the yard. Over successive years family members hear sounds like "like something from the pits of hell screaming" in the nearby woods.
Source: GCBRO

Date: Spring 1976
Witnesses: five unnamed
Location: Around Pembroke, Christian County
Report: Residents of isolated rural homes report three sightings of a six-foot hairy biped with broad shoulders and glowing green eyes.
Sources: BFCU, p. 286; STAAU, p. 223

Date: Summer 1976
Witness: "Donald H."
Location: Clark County
Report: Boy riding his bike along Boone Creek, near Winchester, sees a "hairy monster" between 7 and 8 p.m. A strange smell lingers when his 4 brothers investigate.
Source: BFRO #2381

Date: September 1976
Witness: Unnamed
Location: Panther Creek, Daviess County

Report:	Farmer and his German shepherd flee from bipedal creature described as "big, black and hairy."
Source:	GCBRO

Date:	October 1976
Witness:	Unnamed
Location:	Fort Knox, Meade County
Report:	Young recruit bivouacked in woods on U.S. Army base sees a hairy biped over 6 feet tall at 4:30 a.m.
Source:	GCBRO

Date:	January 1977
Witness:	Unnamed
Location:	Simpson County
Report:	Police officer on night patrol sees Bigfoot cross a highway. Published references to other local sightings provide no details.
Sources:	BFCU, p. 290; STAAU, p. 223

Date:	July 1977
Witnesses:	Two unnamed
Location:	Near Chavies, Perry County
Report:	Boys investigate their pony's agitated behavior at 11:30 p.m. They see an apelike creature 7 to 9 feet tall easily step over a 4-rail fence.
Source:	BFRO #2430

Date:	July 1977
Witnesses:	Two unnamed
Location:	Jeffersontown, Jefferson County
Report:	A couple "star gazing" on Old Taylorsville Road see a white-haired Bigfoot watching their car from 100 feet away.
Source:	GCBRO

Date:	October 1977
Witness:	Unnamed
Location:	Near Jeffersontown, Jefferson County
Report:	Male witness from the July 1977 incident sees the same creature three miles from the original sighting location.
Source:	GCBRO

Date:	1978
Witness:	Unnamed
Location:	Lake Barkley, Trigg County
Report:	Locals discover large humanoid footprints.
Source:	KBF

Date:	July 1978
Witnesses:	Jan Thompson and two cousins
Location:	Grand Rivers, Livingston County
Report:	Children hear howling from the woods, then see a tall bipedal "wolf like creature" with shiny black eyes. One witness claims the beast grabbed him and tore his pants.
Source:	KBF

Date:	August 1978
Witnesses:	Larry Nelson and three companions
Location:	Owensboro, Daviess County
Report:	Residents of Fairview Drive form a "Bigfoot posse" after police ignore their sightings of a biped 8 to 9 feet tall that leaves foot prints 14 to 16 inches long and 6 to 7 inches wide. Four men meet the creature and shoot it three times at close range, but it escapes.
Sources:	BFCU, pp. 302-3; KBF

Date:	August 15, 1978
Witness:	"Matt H."
Location:	Daniel Boone National Forest, Powell County
Report:	Ten-year-old camper smells a foul odor, then sees a hairy biped "as tall as a few of the smaller trees it stood next to."
Source:	BFRO #912

Date:	August 17, 1978
Witness:	Near Campbellsville, Taylor County
Report:	Farmer hears nocturnal screams that "frightened the daylights out of him."
Source:	BFRO #3269

Date:	Autumn 1978
Witnesses:	Two unnamed
Location:	Lockport, Henry County
Report:	Young brothers investigate a disturbance in their barn and see a "very tall, hairy creature" slowly retreating.
Sources:	BFRO #2383; KBF

Date:	December 22, 1978
Witness:	Shirley Elkins
Location:	Paintsville, Johnson County
Report:	During emergency flood evacuation, a hairy "human looking creature" shakes the witness's home, then retreats.
Sources:	IBS #176; KBF

Date:	Late 1970s
Witness:	"Tracey" and three companions
Location:	Hillman Ferry Camping Area, Lyon County
Report:	Bicyclists flee from crashing sounds in the forest.
Source:	KBF

Date:	1979
Witnesses:	four unnamed
Location:	Flat Lick, Knox County
Report:	Boys aged 6 to 12 report seeing a 7-foot hairy primate pass their front yard.
Sources:	GCBRO; KBF

Date:	1979
Witnesses:	Two unnamed
Location:	Lockport, Henry County
Report:	Same brothers from autumn 1978 incident tape screams from nearby woods. A game warden identifies the sound as "mountain lions mating," although cougars are believed extinct in Kentucky.
Source:	BFRO #2383

Date:	1979
Witnesses:	Multiple unnamed
Location:	Hopkins County
Report:	"Three-day flurry of sightings" reported in an unnamed local newspaper, with no further details provided.
Source:	KBF

Date:	Early March 1979
Witnesses:	Several unnamed
Location:	Pennyrile Parkway, Christian County
Report:	Motorists report sightings of a hairy creature seven to eight feet tall on several successive nights.

Sources:	BFCU, p. 305; KBF

Date:	June 1979
Witness:	Vicki Jones
Location:	Big Bone, Boone County
Report:	An unseen prowler shakes the same mobile home later occupied by witnesses Jackie Jones and Dave Stulz (see March-April 1980 below).
Source:	*Creature Chronicles* No. 2

Date:	1980-83
Witnesses:	Unnamed
Location:	Rush Creek, Carter County
Report:	Rural family claims a series of incidents including strange cries, broken trees, slaughtered wildlife, and "an old Indian men looking through the window." Husband claims "around 30" other witnesses but says "they were no help," since "they would not talk about it."
Source:	BFRO #1850

Date:	March 31, 1980
Witness:	Jackie Jones and Dave Stulz
Location:	Big Bone, Boone County
Report:	Witnesses see a 4-foot-tall hairy biped prowling outside their home between 12:30 and 1 a.m.
Source:	*Creature Chronicles* No. 2

Date:	April 1, 1980
Witness:	Jackie Jones and Dave Stulz
Location:	Big Bone, Boone County
Report:	While speaking on the phone to investigators at 12:30 p.m., witnesses see the same creature flee their yard and leap into a nearby river.
Source:	BFCU, p. 308; Creature Chronicles No. 2; KBF

Date:	September 1980
Witness:	Unnamed
Location:	Highway 1137, Harlan County
Report:	Motorist sees a hairy biped 8 to 8.5 feet tall run across the road.
Source:	KBF

Date:	September 9, 1980
Witness:	Unnamed
Location:	Maysville, Fleming County
Report:	Bigfoot allegedly chases a woman around her car in a mall parking lot.
Source:	KBF

Date:	October 4 or 7, 1980
Witnesses:	Charles Fulton and Anna Mae Saunders
Location:	Maysville or Mays Lick, Mason County
Report:	A seven-foot biped with glowing eyes, covered in white hair, steals a chicken and flees when a witness fires gunshots.
Sources:	BFCU, pp. 169, 309; BFRO #2425

Date:	October 10, 1980
Witness:	J.L. Tumey
Location:	Fairview, Fleming County
Report:	A "large dark creature" steals a frozen chicken from an outdoor freezer, then flees as the witness fires gunshots. Police find white

Source:

hairs on the freezer's handle, then locate the dismembered chicken with footprints 12 to 14 inches long and 6 inches wide. BFCU, pp. 169-70; BFRO #2382; IBS #1089 (incorrectly dated from 2000)

Date: November 5, 1980
Witness: "N.C."
Location: Near Maysville, Mason County
Report: Truck driver traveling on U.S. Highway 68 between 4 and 5 a.m. sees a biped 6 to 7 feet tall, covered in white hair.
Sources: BFRO #2426; KBF

Date: January 15, 1981
Witness: Unnamed
Location: Barkley Lake, Trigg County
Report: Police examine a trail of oversized humanoid footprints, finally dismissing the case as a hoax.
Source: KBF

Date: Early 1980s
Witnesses: "Adam" and "Bill"
Location: Land Between the Lakes National Recreation Area
Report: Police officers on midnight patrol see a "werewolf" near the site where a missing child's mutilated body was recovered.
Source: Jan Thompson via KBF

Date: June 1982
Witnesses: Two unnamed
Location: Union County
Report: Brothers fishing at a private farm see something "big, black, and hairy" watching from the forest.
Source: GCBRO

Date: 1983
Witnesses: Four unnamed
Location: Undisclosed
Report: Campers see a biped taller than their 7-foot tent watching them from 100 yards away.
Source: KBF

Date: December 24, 1983
Witness: Jan Thompson
Location: Near Sturgis, Union County
Report: While returning home from Indiana on a snowy night, witness sees an apparent naked man with milky-white skin, surmounted by a monstrous bloody face and long matted scalp hair, emerge from a roadside field.
Source: KBF

Date: Mid-1980s
Witness: Unnamed
Location: Near Owensboro, Daviess County
Report: Motorist sees a muscular biped "with bare spots like it was losing hair" cross the road in front of her car.
Source: GCBRO

Date: January 1984
Witnesses: Two unnamed
Location: Lost Creek, Breathitt County
Report: Children find child-sized bare footprints in the ice of a frozen creek. Their mother then relates a story of her grandmother leav-

ing food scraps outdoors for "the hairy man."

Source:	BFRO #9407; KBF

Date:	May 1984
Witnesses:	Five unnamed
Location:	Owen County
Report:	Hunters track a large hairy biped suspected of "raiding" local farms. Footprints lead into a cave, which proves to be empty, with no other apparent exit.
Source:	KBF

Date:	September 1985
Witnesses:	Four unnamed
Location:	Scott County
Report:	Motorist and passengers see a biped 8 to 9 feet tall with glowing eyes step over a 6-foot roadside fence "without using arms or hand."
Source:	KBF

Date:	July 1986
Witnesses:	Two unnamed
Location:	Coal Harbor Hill, Perry County
Report:	Strollers on a country road hear screams from the woods at 2 a.m. One witness recalls a prior similar incident, date unknown.
Sources:	BFRO #2429; GCBRO; IBS #863; KBF

Date:	Summer 1987
Witnesses:	Six unnamed
Location:	Burbanks Lakes, Henderson County
Report:	Campers hear heavy footsteps in the forest circling their camp.
Source:	KBF

Date:	Summer 1987
Witnesses:	Four unnamed
Location:	Southern Jefferson County
Report:	Friends parked in the woods at midnight hear wild screams and growls, accompanied by snapping branches.
Sources:	GCBRO; KBF

Date:	"Around 1988"
Witnesses:	"Clay" and his mother
Location:	Fedscreek, Pike County
Report:	Woman and her thirteen-year-old son see a large gray-and-black creature moving on all fours, then rising to walk bipedally near their rural home.
Source:	KBF

Date:	1988
Witnesses:	Two unnamed
Location:	Higginson-Henry Wildlife Management Area, Union County
Report:	Hunters flee a large hairy biped.
Source:	KBF

Date:	1988
Witness:	Unnamed
Location:	Henderson County
Report:	Motorist on Ohio River Road sees a brown-haired creature six to seven feet tall run into the woods.
Source:	KBF

Date:	Summer 1988
Witnesses:	Chad Askins and friend

Location:	Ohio County
Report:	Hunters see a "large, dark shape" stooped beside a stream, then rising to stand erect.
Source:	KBF

Date:	Late 1980s
Witnesses:	Two unnamed
Location:	North of Louisa, Lawrence County
Report:	Cousins returning from a nocturnal hunt see a seven-foot hairy biped standing beside Route 23.
Source:	BFE; KBF

Date:	Late 1980s
Witnesses:	Two unnamed
Location:	Near Pilgrim, Martin County
Report:	Nocturnal fishermen flee an eight-foot red-eyed monster, which stops to eat their string of discarded fish. Next morning a neighbor finds his dog mutilated and partially eaten, surrounded by "extremely big" humanoid footprints.
Source:	KBF

Date:	Spring 1990
Witness:	Jan Thompson
Location:	Near Benton, Marshall County
Report:	Commercial courier sees birds and animals flee across Cole Cemetery Road, pursued by "something very tall, very large in width and very strong," emitting "a deep lion's growl." Her customer states that his dog was beheaded by an unseen predator several weeks earlier, but blames a bobcat.
Source:	BFRO #317; KBF

Date:	1991
Witness:	Unnamed
Location:	Cloverport, Breckenridge County
Report:	Resident of M&L Landfill Road reports strange sounds and a "very stinky" smell "like old dead dog."
Source:	KBF

Date:	May 1991
Witness:	Two unnamed
Location:	"Central Kentucky"
Report:	Motorist and passenger traveling on "a north-south highway" at 1 a.m. see a brown-haired biped 7 to 8 feet tall cross the road in front of their car.
Source:	GCBRO

Date:	July 1991
Witnesses:	Two unnamed
Location:	Lewisburg, Logan County
Report:	Father and son arrive home at 9 p.m. and hear loud roars on their property. The son investigates, seeing an eight-foot hairy biped flee through the woods, snapping off branches.
Source:	BFRO #2391; KBF

Date:	September 1991
Witnesses:	Two unnamed
Location:	Ashland, Boyd County
Report:	Nocturnal visitors to a "haunted" bridge see a "massive creature" approaching "somewhat on all fours," then rising to its hind legs. They flee, later estimating the beast's height at sixteen feet.
Source:	KBF

Date:	Autumn 1991
Witnesses:	Two unnamed
Location:	Near Cynthiana, Harrison County
Report:	While driving on a country road at 9 p.m., witnesses see a three-foot-tall biped resembling "a slightly shaggy monkey with lupine legs" cross in front of their car.
Source:	KBF

Date:	Early 1990s
Witnesses:	Two unnamed
Location:	Near Kimper, Pike County
Report:	Teenagers find "very large" humanoid footprints in woods.
Source:	BFRO #4624

Date:	Early 1990s
Witnesses:	Several unnamed
Location:	Henderson County
Report:	Teens parked at an isolated lake hear "terrible screams" and see a large creature swimming with overhand strokes.
Source:	KBF

Date:	Early 1990s
Witness:	Unnamed
Location:	Near Geneva, Henderson County
Report:	Deer hunter sees an eight-foot biped with "frizzy" hair, resembling "a giant hairy Negro."
Source:	KBF

Date:	November 11-15, 1992
Witness:	Two unnamed
Location:	Near Blaine, Lawrence County
Report:	Hunter hears strange sounds in woods, then sees a black biped pass through the woods. A partner finds a large pile of stool with clinging black hairs.
Source:	BFRO #7023

Date:	1993
Witnesses:	Two unnamed
Location:	Christian County
Report:	Driver and passenger see a gray-haired, red-eyed Bigfoot standing beside a rural road at night.
Source:	BFRO #2435

Date:	Mid-January 1993
Witness:	"P.B." and sister
Location:	Highway 121, Ballard County
Report:	While driving from Mayfield to Wickliffe at 2:30 a.m., witnesses see an eight-foot black-haired creature in their headlights.
Sources:	BFRO #2363; IBS #1095 & 3863; KBF

Date:	July 1993
Witness:	Unnamed
Location:	Bear Mountain, Madison County
Report:	Hiker hears tapping sounds, then sees a "huge" biped from 250 yards away, later estimating its height at 7 feet, based on nearby trees.
Sources:	BFRO #2368; IBS #901 & 3352; KBF

Date:	October 1993
Witnesses:	Two unnamed

Location: Near Lawrenceville, Anderson County
Report: Father-son deer hunters glimpse a "very shy" Bigfoot on Bods Mill Road, near "the old Sims farm."
Source: BFRO #10451 KBF

Date: 1993 or 1994
Witnesses: Two unnamed
Location: Lincoln County
Report: Children find "a big footprint" in lakeside mud.
Source: GCBRO

Date: August 1994
Witnesses: "Dawn" and unnamed boyfriend
Location: Near Ashland, Boyd County
Report: A couple driving on I-68 after midnight see a biped seven to eight foot tall, standing beside the highway.
Source: KBF

Date: Mid-October 1994
Witnesses: Eight unnamed
Location: Near Virgie, Pike County
Report: Nocturnal coon hunters see a dark-haired biped 7 to 8 feet tall standing beside an old mining road. They stop and find footprints 15 to 16 inches long, in mud.
Source: BFRO #2435

Date: 1995
Witness: Several unnamed
Location: Constance, Boone County
Report: Residents report strange "yowling" sounds in the woods behind their home.
Source: BFRO #2365

Date: 1995
Witness: Unnamed
Location: Daniel Boone Forest, Morgan County
Report: Hiker sees a biped more than 7 feet tall watching him from 80 yards away. Skeptics call the witness "a known drunk."
Source: KBF

Date: Summer 1995
Witnesses: Two unnamed
Location: Lawrence County
Report: Cousins hear loud, high-pitched sounds near their rural home at night, comparable to supposed Bigfoot audio recordings aired on TV.
Source: BFRO #2389

Date: November 7, 1995
Witnesses: Four unnamed
Location: Lonesome Woods, Hopkins County
Report: "Weird moaning" disturbs campers, at 9 p.m. One goes to relieve himself at 10:30 and meets an 8-foot primate drinking from a stream. All four witnesses see the beast run away, making sounds comparable to a truck driving over branches.
Sources: BFRO #2384; KBF

Date: 1996
Witnesses: Bart Nunnelly and companion
Location: Near Unionville, Union County

Report:	Investigators visit the Slack Farm on Dike Road, where Nunnelly reports a "long tradition" of sightings involving a 10-foot apelike creature. They find 10 freshly-dismembered pigs and report a sense of being watched.
Source:	KBF

Date:	October 1996
Witnesses:	Two unnamed
Location:	Barkley Lake, Trigg County
Report:	Friends poaching mussels at night hear a "yawning holler," then see an eight-foot-tall biped emerge from the woods, hurling a log against their car.
Source:	BFRO #12641

Date:	November 1996
Witnesses:	Three unnamed
Location:	Uniontown, Union County
Report:	Motorist sees a biped 9 to 10 feet tall cross Dike Road in front of her truck between 1 and 2 a.m. Her husband and son, commercial fishermen, hear "log breaking noises" at the same location for weeks afterward.
Source:	BFRO #11998

Date:	1997
Witness:	"Nancy"
Location:	Rockholds, Whitley County
Report:	Bipedal creature 8 feet tall and 4 feet wide, covered with reddish-brown hair 6-8 inches long, approaches the teenage witness while she is cutting trees near her rural home.
Source:	KBF

Date:	July 12, 1997
Witnesses:	Harry Hardin, "Clark" and several others
Location:	Devils Jump, McCreary County
Report:	Witnesses see a tan-colored biped 7 to 8 feet tall wading across the Cumberland River. Subsequently, 15 miles away, they find a "dome structure made from sticks."
Source:	IBS #2882

Date:	October 4, 1997
Witnesses:	Two unnamed
Location:	Near Shady Grove, Crittenden County
Report:	Father and son hear an "awful noise" in the woods but "didn't think anything of it."
Source:	BFRO #2367

Date:	1997-98
Witnesses:	Three unnamed
Location:	Carter County
Report:	Son and daughter of the Rush Creek witness from 1980-83, with his son's girlfriend, report a Bigfoot sighting. No further details available.
Source:	BFRO #1850

Date:	1998
Witnesses:	1 unnamed
Location:	Near Lake Cumberland, Clinton County
	11-year-old girl sees an 8.5-foot biped prowling outside her home on a foggy night, at 2:00 a.m.
Source:	BFE

Date:	1998
Witness:	Unnamed
Location:	Mayfield, Graves County
	A sound of breaking limbs precedes the nocturnal sighting of a large black primate with glowing red eyes.
Source:	KBF

Date:	1998
Witnesses:	Unnamed
Location:	Mayfield, Graves County
Report:	Man dumping tree limbs in the woods behind his house at night meets a bipedal creature over six feet tall, with "small red eyes" and a "bad smell."
Source:	GCBRO

Date:	January 1998
Witnesses:	Several unnamed
Location:	Near Shady Grove, Crittenden County
Report:	Witness to an October 1997 sighting returns to the area with friends. They see a red-eyed biped 6 feet 10 inches tall, 100 yards distant in thick woods at night.
Source:	BFRO #2367

Date:	March 3, 1998
Witness:	"Doug"
Location:	Firebrick, Lewis County
Report:	Rural resident hears strange sounds near his home and finds "snapped trees on old ones and new ones."
Source:	OBSG

Date:	March 5, 1998
Witnesses:	"Dallas," "Danny" and "Doug"
Location:	Firebrick, Lewis County
Report:	OBSG investigators visit scene of March 3 incident and hear "two sounds that we knew Bigfoot makes." They also photograph "slide marks" in mud. Dallas "felt like Bigfoot was in this area but did not feel that he lived there."
Source:	OBSG

Date:	August 1998
Witnesses:	"Wayne" and "Tim"
Location:	Lloyd Ridge, Wayne County
Report:	Motorist parked in a van sees Bigfoot cross the road. Report dated August 17 mentions photos but fails to describe them.
Source:	OBSG

Date:	August 1998
Witnesses:	Several unnamed
Location:	Shady Grove, Crittenden County
Report:	Residents of Blackburn Church Road report multiple sightings of a seven-foot red-eyed creature.
Source:	KBF

Date:	August 1998
Witnesses:	Two unnamed
Location:	Ashland, Boyd County
Report:	Mother and son returning from the hospital at 2:45 a.m. see a long-haired biped cross the road in two strides, narrowly avoiding collision with their car.
Source:	BFRO #3253; KBF

Date:	August 10, 1998
Witnesses:	Several unnamed
Location:	Crittenden County
Report:	While riding with his sisters and some friends, a witness to the October 1997 sighting glimpses a large biped from thirty yards.
Source:	BFRO #2367

Date:	September 10, 1998
Witnesses:	Two unnamed
Location:	Jefferson County Forest
Report:	Joggers hear moaning sounds and branches snapping, then see a bipedal creature 7 to 8 feet tall, weighing 400+ pounds, from a range of 100 yards.
Sources:	GCBRO; KBF

Date:	1999
Witness:	Unnamed
Location:	Near Baskett, Henderson County
Report:	Motorist sees two brown bipeds standing in a bean field beside Highway 60.
Source:	KBF

Date:	July 1999
Witness:	"Brad"
Location:	Davenport Bay, Lake Barkley, Lyon County
Report:	Witness glimpses a biped with "an hourglass figure" like a "young female" running through woods.
Source:	KBF

Date:	July 14, 1999
Witnesses:	Several unnamed
Location:	Knox County
Report:	Campers wake to "running" sounds and a "rotten" odor at 1 a.m., then glimpse a manlike figure 7 to 8 feet tall, making a "grumbling noise."
Source:	GCBRO

Date:	August 4, 1999
Witnesses:	Two unnamed
Location:	Near Lake Cumberland, Clinton County
Report:	Siblings walking through woods at 2 a.m. see an eight-foot creature with "big eyes" shaking a tree, as if "to get something down from it." The female witness reported a prior sighting in 1998.
Sources:	BFE; KBF

Date:	Autumn 1999 or 2000
Witness:	Unnamed
Location:	Interstate 75, Grant County
Report:	Motorist driving from Cincinnati to Winchester, Kentucky, sees a dark-colored biped over 6 feet tall, with an "angry demeanor," cross the highway around 1:30 a.m.
Source:	BFRO #8715

Date:	May 1, 2000
Witness:	Unnamed
Location:	Near Eddyville, Lyon County
Report:	Motorist nearly collides with a snarling "huge beast" at 10:30 p.m.
Source:	GCBRO

Date:	Late July/early August 2000
Witnessed:	Two unnamed
Location:	Near Mortons Gap, Hopkins County
Report:	While fishing, a couple hear "loud scraping noises" in the woods. Retreating to their truck, they are attacked by a shrieking biped that strikes the vehicle three times.
Source:	KBF

Date:	Early September 2000
Witness:	Joanna Carter
Location:	Highway 1137, Harlan County
Report:	Motorist sees an apelike biped over eight feet tall walking along the highway, retreating into a berry patch. She stops and collects "long and nappy" hair samples, but refuses to submit them for scientific testing.
Source:	BFE

Date:	November 2000
Witness:	"B"
Location:	Wildcat Road, Anderson County
Report:	Deer hunter hears crashing sounds in the woods, followed by the "scariest scream I have ever heard...like the whistle of a train."
Source:	KBF

Date:	November 11, 2000
Witness:	Unnamed
Location:	Princeton, Caldwell County
Report:	GCBRO researchers list a noontime sighting, then delete it from their database, reporting it "unclear as to whether it is true or not."
Source:	GCBRO

Date:	January 4, 2001
Witness:	Unnamed
Location:	Near Greenup, Greenup County
Report:	Motorist on U.S. Highway 23 reports nocturnal sighting of a creature 8 feet tall, weighing about 450 pounds.
Sources:	BFRO #1265; KBF.

Date:	February 2, 2001
Witnesses:	Two unnamed
Location:	Near Louellen, Harlan County
Report:	Men driving to work at night see a seven-foot hairy biped rooting through roadside trash, then fleeing across the road.
Source:	BFRO #10556

Date:	Mid-February 2001
Witness:	One unnamed
Location:	Near Louellen, Harlan County
Report:	Nocturnal motorist passing the site of the February 2 incident sees "the same thing" cross Highway 119.
Source:	BFRO #10556

Date:	Late March or early April 2001
Witness:	Unnamed
Location:	Near Lake Barkley, Trigg County
Report:	Bigfoot researcher hears strange howling in the woods near a friend's home. Subsequently, his "encounters of Bigfoot activity seemed to increase," but he provides no details.
Source:	KBF

Date:	November 2001
Witness:	Unnamed
Location:	Crab Orchard, Lincoln County
Report:	Deer hunter hears grunting sounds, then sees "something big and black" rise from all fours to stand upright. The creature throws a stick "at something in a tree."
Source:	GCBRO

Date:	November 7, 2001
Witness:	Unnamed
Location:	Near Hazard, Breathitt County
Report:	Motorist sees an apelike creature 8 to 9 feet tall cross the road, then stops and finds 20-inch footprints.
Source:	GCBRO

Date:	2002
Witness:	Unnamed
Location:	Spencer County
Report:	Rural resident claims two nocturnal Bigfoot sightings, several days apart. On the first occasion, a "stocky" Bigfoot with "a skinnier lower body" drops fifteen feet from a tree near the observer's home, then walks into the forest. A third sighting occurs "less than a month" after the prior incidents.
Source:	GCBRO

Date:	2002
Witness:	"Joey" and unnamed coworker
Location:	Bell County, near Know County line
Report:	Witnesses en route to work see a large, dark-haired biped cross Highway 25.
Source:	KBF

Date:	Late 2002
Witnesses:	"Jeremiah" and three companions
Location:	Between Maysville and Germantown
Report:	Motorist and passengers see a hairy biped 6 to 7 feet tall cross Highway 435 at 10:30 p.m.
Source:	KBF

Date:	Early 2003
Witnesses:	"Jeremiah" and brother
Location:	Near Maysville, Mason County
Report:	Witness from the previous incident sees a similar creature on Clyde T. Barbour Highway, near the location of his prior sighting.
Source:	KBF

Date:	2003
Witness:	Unnamed
Location:	Spencer County
Report:	Rural resident claims a fourth nocturnal Bigfoot sighting near his home.
Source:	GCBRO

Date:	2003
Witness:	Unnamed
Location:	Near Ashland, Carter County
Report:	Motorist saw a "brown upright thing" six to seven feet tall cross the highway in front of his car.
Source:	KBF

Date:	February 20, 2003
Witness:	Unnamed
Location:	Between Pine Knot and Williamsburg
Report:	Motorist sees a seven-foot biped covered with gray hair, crossing Highway 92.
Sources:	BFRO #5881; GCBRO

Date:	June 24, 2003
Witnesses:	Several unnamed
Location:	Kenton County
Report:	While visiting an unnamed park, witnesses notice a "very unique smell of sour meat and wet hair," then see a biped "maybe nine feet tall."
Source:	GCBRO

Date:	June 30, 2003
Witnesses:	Four unnamed
Location:	Diamond Resort, Barren County
Report:	Family on vacation hears cries from the forest like "that of a women being brutalized and screaming as a result."
Source:	BFRO #6632

Date:	July 2003
Witnesses:	Two unnamed
Location:	Near Blaine, Lawrence County
Report:	Gensing hunters meet an reddish-brown apelike creature 6 to 7 feet tall, with 4-foot-wide shoulders, exuding odor "like a cross between a skunk and a wet dog." A week later, one witness sees the creature watching her home from 70 to 100 feet away.
Source:	BFRO #11966; KBF

Date:	Summer 2003 or 2004
Witnesses:	"Valerie" and husband
Location:	Near Parker's Lake, McCreary County
Report:	Campers in a mobile home wake on two successive nights to strange screams "like a peacock's cry" from nearby woods.
Source:	KBF

Date:	2004
Witnesses:	Two members of Garcia family
Location:	Cold Springs, Campbell County
Report:	Residents wake to sounds outside their home. Father and son-in-law see Bigfoot prowling in the yard.
Source:	KBF

Date:	April 20, 2004
Witness:	Unnamed
Location:	Near Stanton, Powell County
Report:	Witness walking home at 2:30 a.m. smells an indescribable "bad odor," then sees a dark-haired biped six to seven foot tall splash across a nearby stream.
Source:	BFRO #8517

Date:	June 2004
Witnesses:	Two unnamed
Location:	Trigg County
Report:	Motorist and passenger see a Bigfoot seven to eight foot tall standing beside a rural road at night.
Source:	KBF

Date:	November 2004
Witness:	Unnamed

Location:	Blaine, Lawrence County
Report:	Witness from July 2003 ginseng-hunting encounter blames Bigfoot for killing and mutilating "several" dogs, and for lobbing rocks at the witness.
Source:	BFRO #11966

Date:	December 2004 (first week)
Witness:	"M.A.B."
Location:	Bell County
Report:	Nocturnal motorist on Highway 461 sees a "huge boulder with hair" beside highway, accompanied by "a gagging smell." She denies striking the object but later finds unidentified "hair hanging off my tail pipe."
Source:	KBF

Date:	January 21, 2005
Witness:	Unnamed
Location:	Spencer County
Report:	Witness claims a fifth Bigfoot sighting within three years, near his rural home.
Source:	GCBRO

Date:	July 2005
Witness:	Unnamed
Location:	State Route 164 near Canton, Trigg County
Report:	Motorist observes a hairy biped "at least 10 feet tall," standing beside highway at 8:30 a.m.
Source:	BFRO #13289

Date:	July 14, 2005
Witness:	Adam Candler
Location:	Spottsville, Henderson County
Report:	Motorist sees a hairy biped seven to eight feet tall crossing Green River Road. Candler later told Bart Nunnelly that two relatives and a friend had seen similar creatures at different times, but provided no dates or details.
Source:	KBF

Date:	July 23, 2005
Witness:	Unnamed
Location:	Warren County
Report:	Hiker sees a large hairy biped with "human-like eyes and a bad smell" chasing a deer through the woods.
Sources:	GCBRO; KBF

Date:	January 2006
Witness:	"Mark"
Location:	Trigg County, near Tennessee border
Report:	Motorist driving to Tennessee at 10:30 p.m. reports seeing a Bigfoot "the size of a mountain lion" crawling along the highway with "a lizard-like motion," resembling a man doing push-ups.
Source:	KBF

Date:	May 2006
Witnesses:	"Matt" and three companions
Location:	Morehead, Rowan County
Report:	Motorist and passengers see a seven-foot shaggy creature beside the road at 2 p.m.
Source:	KBF

Date:	May 24, 2006
Witnesses:	"Clyde" and three companions
Location:	Near Inez, Martin County
Report:	"Groaning sounds" disturb campers at 3 a.m. They see an apelike creature 7 to 8 feet tall, watching from 15 feet away and "looking startled."
Source:	KBF

Date:	May 25, 2006
Witnesses:	"Lon" and 14 companions
Location:	Buck Creek, Martin County
Report:	Loud sounds and a "horrible stench" wake campers at 2 a.m. A hairy biped eight to nine feet tall, with "piercing red eyes," flees after witness fires pistol shots.
Source:	KBF

Date:	June 4, 2006
Witnesses:	"Aaron," "Dustin" and "Neil"
Location:	Near Ermine, Letcher County
Report:	Campers wake to screeching sounds at 1 a.m., then see a biped 7 to 8 feet tall cross a grassy field "running like no man could run."
Source:	KBF

Date:	June 7, 2006
Witnesses:	"Rick" & companion
Location:	Highway 536 near Independence, Kenton County
Report:	Motorist narrowly avoids striking a seven-foot hairy biped as it crosses the road at 11:30 p.m.
Source:	KBF

Date:	June 27, 2006
Witnesses:	"Andy" and "Jeremy"
Location:	Near Mount Vernon, Rockcastle County
Report:	Bigfoot six to eight feet tall watches witnesses set off fireworks.
Source:	KBF

Date:	July 2, 2006
Witness:	"Josh"
Location:	Bon Harbor Hills, Daviess County
Report:	Bigfoot, seven to nine feet tall, lobs a rock at the witness, grazing his ear and smashing a crude "teepee" structure. Same witness heard loud, unexplained screams in the area several months earlier.
Source:	KBF

Date:	July 9, 2006
Witnesses:	"Taylor" and three companions
Location:	Cave Run Lake Marina, Rowan County
Report:	Witnesses watch an eight-foot hairy biped drinking water, then hear its "really loud and distinctive scream."
Source:	KBF

Dates:	August 2006 to March 29, 2007
Witnesses:	Several unnamed
Location:	Simpson County
Report:	Farm residents report "several" encounters with "a large, white, hairy, clawed, and horned type gorilla" on their property.
Source:	GCBRO

Date:	October 2006
Witnesses:	Josh Sparks and son
Location:	Greenfield Road near Ashland, Boyd County

Report:	Hikers searching the woods for "tree breaks and teepees" meet a 7.5-foot hairy biped with an "outdoor odor."
Source:	KBF

Date:	November 5, 2006
Witnesses:	Two unnamed
Location:	Red River Gorge, Powell County
Report:	Campers flee from ominous sounds, a "rancid ferret smell," and glowing red eyes four feet above the forest floor.
Source:	KBF

Date:	November 6, 2006
Witnesses:	"Gene" and two friends
Location:	Near Martha, Lawrence County
Report:	While hiking in woods, witness demonstrates stick-knocking noises heard the previous night. Identical sounds emanate from the forest, with loud "whooping" cries.
Source:	KBF

Date:	November 14, 2006
Witnesses:	"Chris" and companion
Location:	Fort Thomas, Campbell County
Report:	Witnesses hear sounds in woods near their home at 11:30 p.m., then see hairy biped 4 to 5 feet tall.
Source:	KBF

Date:	December 5, 2006
Witness:	"Aaron"
Location:	Near Lawrenceburg, Lawrence County
Report:	Deer hunter reports "a terrible skunk smell" and loud growling, lasting ten minutes.
Source:	KBF

Date:	Autumn 2006
Witness:	"Josh"
Location:	Bridge Hollow Road, Allen County
Report:	Motorist returning home from Barren River Lake sees a biped seven to eight feet tall, with "long mangy hair" and visible male genitalia cross a roadside creek bed.
Source:	KBF

Date:	January 3, 2007
Witness:	"Chris"
Location:	Lazy Acre Estates, Barren County
Report:	Hunter observes foul-smelling Bigfoot while dismantling his deer stand at 4 a.m., near Cave City.
Source:	KBF
Date:	January 23, 2007
Witnesses:	Two unnamed
Location:	Near Catlettsburg, Boyd County
Report:	After "many" disturbances by unseen nocturnal prowlers, husband and wife find and photograph large tracks outside their house.
Source:	KBF

Date:	March 28, 2007
Witness:	Brad Law and girlfriend
Location:	Nebo, Hopkins County
Report:	Couple driving on Rose Creek Road see a "dark object" lying beside the road, rising to walk on all fours, then flee on two legs.
Source:	KBF

Date: April 25, 2007
Witness: "Jordan"
Location: Near Mt. Sterling, Montgomery County
Report: Witness walking near his rural home sees a red-eyed biped
             with horns, white fur, and a long black tail.
Source: KBF

Date: May 7, 2007
Witness: Unnamed
Location: Barren County
Report: A hunter sees a "hunched over," foul-smelling eight-foot biped
             with hair "about the color of tree bark."
Source: GCBRO

Date: January 27, 2008
Witness: Dakota Poff
Location: Bluegrass Estates, Danville, Boyle County
Report: While walking near home at 2 p.m., witness sees an eight-foot
             biped with black hair and "coal-black eyes."
Source: KBF

Date: April to November 2008
Witnesses: Several unnamed
Location: Eastern Lewis County
Report: Farmer and his children claim multiple sightings of a
             foul-smelling hairy biped, blamed for missing livestock.
Source: BFRO #24976

Witness: Pam Lovins and two companions
Location: Daniel Boone National Forest, Rowan County
Report: A BFRO investigator from West Virginia interviews two recent
             Bigfoot witnesses, then accompanies them to the scene of their
             sighting, where she reportedly catches an unknown primate on
             videotape.
Source: BFRO #24674

Date: August 10, 2008
Witness: "Suzy"
Location: Near Russell, Greenup County
Report: Witness reports crashing sounds and growling in woods near her
             home on two consecutive nights.
Source: KBF

Date: August 16, 2008
Witnesses: "George" and unnamed friend
Location: Near Dover, Mason County
Report: Squirrel hunters claim daylight sighting of an eight-foot hairy
             biped, "really muscular."
Source: KBF

Date: August 17, 2008
Witness: "Grant"
Location: Near Augusta, Bracken County
Report: Lone squirrel hunter meets an eight-foot biped, "really built,"
             with reddish-brown hair and visible male genitalia.
Source: KBF

Date: October 2008
Witnesses: "Ricky" and three unnamed
Location: Near Evarts, Harlan County
Report: Off-road ATV riders sight a black bear, followed by discovery of
             "very large footprints" on dirt road.

Source:	BFRO #25257
Date:	October 17, 2008
Witnesses:	"Ben" and three unnamed friends
Location:	Near Springfield, Washington County
Report:	Young "snipe hunters" dodge flying rocks and sticks, then see a dark-haired biped crouching in woods at 2 a.m.
Source:	KBF
Date:	October 21-22, 2008
Witnesses:	Two unnamed
Location:	Near Slade, Powell County
Report:	Campers hear "really loud howling sounds" at night and photograph "strange tracks" the next morning.
Source:	BFRO #24948
Date:	November 6, 2008
Witnesses:	"Ryan," wife, and unnamed friend
Location:	Alexandria, Campbell County
Report:	While watching TV at night, witnesses hear "screeching" from nearby woods, and crashing sounds as "something big runs down the hill."
Source:	KBF
Date:	Autumn 2008
Witness:	"Clay"
Location:	Near Pikeville, Pike County
Report:	Witness from a 1988 encounter sees a slender bipedal creature with a "dog-shaped head and long ears" outside parents' rural home.
Source:	KBF
Undated:	("many years before" 1978)
Witness:	Unnamed
Location:	Lockport, Henry County
Report:	Witness reports "something" lobbing large stones at him "with great force."
Source:	BFRO #2383
Undated:	("years after" 1965)
Witness:	Unnamed
Location:	Casey County
Report:	Farmer repairing a fence flees from a "bear" walking on its hind legs.
Source:	GCBRO; KBF
Undated:	(after 1998)
Witness:	Unnamed
Location:	Boyd County
Report:	Adult witness from August 1998 Ashland sighting claims "several" subsequent Bigfoot encounters but offers no details.
Source:	BFRO #3523
Undated:	—
Witness:	James Vincent
Location:	Black Hollow, Cumberland County
Report:	Albino, foul-smelling Bigfoot leaves fifteen-inch tracks.
Source:	IBS #439
Undated:	—
Witness:	Unnamed
Location:	Near Owensboro, Daviess County

Report:	Nocturnal sighting by a female motorist.
Source:	GCBRO

Undated:	—
Witnesses:	Two unnamed
Location:	Burbank Lakes, Henderson County
Report:	Loud noises on the lake shore trap two fishermen in their boat overnight, then subside at dawn, allowing them to flee.
Source:	KBF

Undated:	—
Witness:	Unnamed
Location:	Casey County
Report:	Witness from the 1960 drive-in movie sighting above claims a previous Bigfoot encounter during childhood.
Source:	GCBRO

Undated:	—
Witness:	Unnamed
Location:	Greenup County
Report:	Truck driver sees a bipedal creature seven to eight feet tall beside the AA Highway.
Source:	GCBRO

Undated:	—
Witness:	Unnamed
Location:	Perry County
Report:	Motorist sees a biped seven to eight feet tall standing beside a rural highway.
Sources:	KBF

Undated:	—
Witness:	Unnamed
Location:	Carter Caves State Resort Park, Carter County
Report:	Anonymous Bigfoot researcher claims "at least 12 encounters" with Bigfoot, including an albino specimen 9.5 feet tall.
Source:	KBF

Undated:	—
Witness:	Unnamed
Location:	Near Hawesville, Hancock County
Report:	Night watchman at a rural paper mill meets a "tall, dark, hair-covered figure" on his rounds.
Source:	KBF

Date:	"Last week in May," year unknown
Witness:	"Sharon"
Location:	Between Columbia and Knifley, Adair County
Report:	Witness sees creature resembling "a big man covered in hair" while walking dogs in woods nedaer her home.
Source:	KBF

End Notes

Introduction

1. Arthur Cotterell, *The Macmillan Illustrated Encyclopedia of Myths & Legends.* New York: Macmillan, 1989.
2. Newton, *Encyclopedia of Cryptozoology,* p. 3.
3. Ibid., p. 6.
4. Arment, *Cryptozoology,* p. 16.

Chapter 1

1. Kentucky Department of Fish and Wildlife Resources, Species Information; University of Kentucky Department of Entomology, Kentucky Critter Files; Kentucky Exotic Pest Plant Council.
2. Australia Museum Online, "Why most animals are insects."
3. University of Kentucky Department of Entomology, Kentucky Critter Files.
4. "Asian tiger mosquito," Pests and Diseases Image Library, http://www.padil.gov.au/viewPestDiagnosticImages. aspx?id=8; U.S. Department of Agriculture, National Invasive Species Information Center.
5. Kentucky Department of Fish and Wildlife Resources, Species Information; U.S. Department of Agriculture, National Invasive Species Information Center.
6. Kentucky Department of Fish and Wildlife Resources, Species Information; U.S. Department of Agriculture, National Invasive Species Information Center.
7. Todd Koel, Kevin Irons and Eric Ratcliff. "Asian carp invasion of the upper Mississippi River system." Upper Midwest Environmental Sciences Center, November 2000; Kentucky Department of Fish and Wildlife Resources, Species Information; U.S. Department of Agriculture, National Invasive Species Information Center.
8. Koel, Irons and Ratcliff, "Asian carp invasion"; Kentucky Department of Fish and Wildlife Resources, Species Information; U.S. Department of Agriculture, National Invasive Species Information Center.
9. W.R. Courtenay Jr. and J.D. Williams. "Snakeheads (Pisces, Channidae): A biological synopsis and risk assessment," U.S. Geological Survey Circular 1251, 204; U.S. Department of Agriculture, National Invasive Species Information Center.
10. Courtenay and Williams, "Snakeheads"; U.S. Department of Agriculture, National Invasive Species Information Center.
11. Kentucky Department of Fish and Wildlife Resources, "Snakehead found in west Kentucky"; U.S. Fish and Wildlife Service, "Snakehead stories."
12. Kentucky Department of Fish and Wildlife Resources, Species Information.
13. Kentucky Department of Fish and Wildlife Resources, Species Information; Conant and Collins, Reptiles & Amphibians of Eastern/Central North America, pp. 442-3.
14. Kentucky Department of Fish and Wildlife Resources, Species Information; Conant and Collins, pp. 468, 471-2, 481-2, 485-7.
15. Kentucky Department of Fish and Wildlife Resources, Species Information; Conant and Collins, pp. 514, 529-30, 560.
16. Kentucky Department of Fish and Wildlife Resources, Species Information.
17. Kentucky Department of Fish and Wildlife Resources, Species Information; Conant and Collins, pp. 178-9, 180, 185.
18. Kentucky Department of Fish and Wildlife Resources, Species Information; Conant and Collins, pp. 268-9.
19. Kentucky Department of Fish and Wildlife Resources, Species Information; Conant and Collins, pp. 293-5,306-8, 330-1, 333-4, 339, 357-9, 370-1, 375, 397-9.
20. "Kentucky man finds python in rental car," Boston Globe, May 29, 2006.
21. "Hunt for escaped alligator called off," UPI, September 8, 2005; "Missing Alligator Found," WTVF-TV, September 9, 2005; Lisa Dunbar, "An alligator never makes a good pet"; "Captain Chaos gets new home in South Carolina."
22. Kentucky Department of Fish and Wildlife Resources, Species Information; National Geographic Field Guide to Birds of North America, p. 358.
23. Kentucky Department of Fish and Wildlife Resources, Species Information; National Geographic Field Guide to Birds of North America, pp. 42, 182; Kentucky Ornithological Society, Reports of Rare Species to the Kentucky Bird Records Committee.
24. Kentucky Department of Fish and Wildlife Resources, Species Information; American Wild Boar; U.S. Department of Agriculture, National Invasive Species Information Center; Kentucky Wild Boar.
25. Shalia Dewan, "DNA tests to reveal if possible record-size boar is a pig in a poke," *San Francisco Chronicle*, March 19, 2005; Evidence of Manipulation of Stone Feral Hog Shooting Photographs, http://66.226.75.96/pig.
26. Newton, *Florida's Unexpected Wildlife*, p. 2.

27. Kentucky Bigfoot.
28. Ibid.
29. Ibid.; Coleman, *Mysterious America*, pp. 184-5.
30. Coleman, *Mysterious America*, pp. 184-7.

Chapter 2

1. Weissengruber, G.E., G. Forstenpointner, G. Peters, A. Kübber-Heiss, and W.T. Fitch. "Hyoid apparatus and pharynx in the lion (Panthera leo), jaguar (Panthera onca), tiger (Panthera tigris), cheetah (Acinonyx jubatus) and domestic cat (Felis silvestris f. catus)." Journal of Anatomy 201 (September 2002): 195–209.
2. Newton, *Encyclopedia of Cryptozoology*, p. 16.
3. Wilson, Don, and Dee Ann Reeder, *Mammal Species of the World 3rd ed.* (Baltimore: Johns Hopkins University Press, 2005), pp. 544–45.
4. Barbour and Davis, p. 309; Potter; Kentucky Dept. of Fish and Wildlife Resources (hereafter "DFWR"), Species Information, http://fw.ky.ov/kfwis/speciesInfo/speciesList.asp?page=23&strGroup=1&strTaxonomic=&strKey=&strSort1= CommonName&strSort2=ScientificName&strSort3=Class; KDWFR, Transportation and Holding of Native Wildlife, http://fw.ky.gov/transnativeinfo.asp.
5. Shuker, p. 156; Eastern Puma Research Network (hereafter EPRN), undated publications; John Lutz email to the author, Aug. 9, 2007.
6. Crawford, "State wants to know."
7. Ibid.
8. DFWR memo dated Oct. 16, 1996.
9. DFWR memo dated May 1, 1989.
10. DFWR memo dated Nov. 9, 1990.
11. Mandl.
12. Ibid.
13. Crawford, "Mountain lion makes foray."
14. Marcus Cope memorandum, Feb. 9, 1994.
15. DFWR memo dated April 11, 1994.
16. DFWR memo dated Sept. 26, 1995.
17. DFWR memo dated Nov. 20, 1995.
18. DFWR memo dated Dec. 5, 1995.
19. Butz, p. 13.
20. "Local Cougar Sightings."
21. Whitehead.
22. Ibid.
23. Crawford, "Mountain lion reports"; MacArthur; "Are mountain lions attacking pets in Kentucky?"; "Mountain lion on the loose?"
24. "It's some big cat"; "Local Cougar Sightings."
25. Potter; "Mountain lion sightings in northern Kentucky."
26. Ford.
27. Shuker, pp. 28-30, 162-3.
28. Nunnelly, *Mysterious Kentucky*, p. 136; John Lutz, personal email to the author, Aug. 9, 2007; EPRN.
29. Nunnelly, *Mysterious Kentucky*, pp. 136-8; DFWR, Species Information, http://fw.ky.gov/kfwis/speciesInfo/speciesList.asp.
30. John Lutz email, Aug. 9, 2007; Gulf Coast Bigfoot Research Organization (hereafter GCBRO).
31. Crawford, "Sightings spur man's search"; Marcus Cope memorandum, Feb. 9, 1994.
32. DFWR memos dated March 10 and Aug. 17, 1995.
33. John Lutz email, Aug. 9, 2007; Bigfoot Field Researchers Organization (hereafter BFRO), Report No. 3269; Brian Peck, "Ky. black panther," Cryptozoology.com, http://www.cryptozoology.com/sightings/sightings_show.php?id=437; "Local Cougar Sightings"; Mary Nelson email to the author, July 24, 2007.
34. EPRN; Crawford, "Sightings spur man's search"; Nunnelly, *Mysterious Kentucky*, p. 136.
35. "Alabama black panther or just a black cougar?" Cryptozoology.com, http://www.cryptozoology.com/forum/topic_view_thread.php?td=3&pid=521117; Coleman, *Mysterious America*, pp. 127-59.
36. Coleman and Clark, *Creatures of the Outer Edge*, p. 122; Shuker, p. 174.
37. Coleman and Clark, *Creatures*, p. 122.
38. Nunnelly, *Mysterious Kentucky*, p. 138.
39. Coleman, *Mothman*, p. 141; Coleman and Clark, *Creatures*, p. 217; Loren Coleman email to the author, March 16, 2008; Nunnelly, *Mysterious Kentucky*, p. 143.
40. Barbara Rosenman, letter to the author, Oct. 3, 2007; Don Wilson and DeeAnn Reeder, *Mammal Species of the World 3rd ed.* (Baltimore: Johns Hopkins University Press, 2005), pp. 535, 540; Velley Stables & Exotic Livestock, http://www.valleystables-exotics.com.

Chapter 3

1. DFWR, Species Information.
2. Conant and Collins, p. 143.
3. Coleman, *Mysterious America*, pp. 299-304.
4. Cox; Dunbar.
5. "Hunt for escaped alligator called off"; "Missing alligator found."
6. Mardis and Shmidheiser, "Giant gator"; White, "Giant alligator."
7. Mardis and Shmidheiser; White.
8. Coleman, *Mysterious America*, pp. 299-304.
9. DFWR, Species Information; Conant and Collins, pp. 250, 262, 276.
10. "Canip Monster is sighted again"; "Monster still sought."
11. Clark, *Unexplained!*, p. 327; Coleman, *Mothman*, p. 93; Rosales.
12. "Canip Monster is sighted again," *Trimble County Banner*, July 31, 1975; "Monster still sought," *Trimble County*

Banner, August 7, 1975; Eric Pianka, Dennis King and Ruth King, *Varanoid Lizards of the World*. Bloomington: Indiana University Press, 2004; Arment, "Dinos in the U.S.A."
13. Arment, "Dinos in the U.S.A."; Chris Woodyard, Haunted Ohio II, (Beavercreek, OH: Kestrel Publications, 1992), pp. 95-96.
14. Kentucky Bigfoot website (herafter KBF).
15. DFWR, Species Information; Conant and Collins, pp. 342, 363, 408.
16. Nunnelly, *Mysterious Kentucky*, p. 141.
17. Arment, *Boss Snakes*, p. 175.
18. Ibid., pp. 369-70.
19. Ibid., p. 176.
20. Ibid., pp. 370-1; USA Place Names, http://www.placenames.com/us.
21. Arment, *Boss Snakes*, p. 371.
22. Ibid., p. 176.
23. Ibid., p. 176.
24. Ibid., pp. 176-7; Hall, "Giant snakes," p. 27.
25. Arment, *Boss Snakes*, pp. 176-8.
26. Andrew Honigman, associate editor of *Fate*, email to the author dated Jan. 1, 2008; Curtis Fuller, "More and More," *Fate* 16 (December 1965): 22; Hall, "Giant snakes," p. 28; Graham Troop email to the author, July 3, 2007.
27. Nunnelly, *Mysterious Kentucky*, pp. 140-1.
28. Andrew Revkin, "A movable beast: Asian pythons thrive in Florida," *International Herald Tribune*, July 23, 2007; "Kentucky man finds python in rental car."

Chapter 4

1. Eberhart, pp. 655, 674-89.
2. Ward.
3. Ibid.
4. Ibid.
5. Nunnelly, *Mysterious Kentucky*, p. 25.
6. Ernst and Barbour, pp. 117, 255-7; Conant and Collins, p. 148.
7. Oliver Hay, *The Fossil Turtles of North America*. Carnegie Institution of Washington, Publication No. 75, 1908.
8. Nunnelly, *Mysterious Kentucky*, p. 26-7; Sloughs Wildlife Management Area Trail, http://www.trails.com/tcatalog_trail.asp?trailid=HGD128-069.
9. Nunnelly, *Mysterious Kentucky*, pp. 26-7.
10. "Green River," in *The Kentucky Encyclopedia*, http://www.kyenc.org; Nunnelly, *Mysterious Kentucky*, p. 29; Mammoth Cave Online, http://www.mammothcave.com/outdoor.htm.
11. Nunnelly, *Mysterious Kentucky*, pp. 29-30.
12. Ibid., p. 30.
13. The Cephalopod Page, http://www.thecephalopodpage.org; CephBase, http://www.cephbase.utmb.edu.
14. Arment and LaGrange, pp. 47-8.
15. Ibid., p. 48.
16. Newton, *Strange Indiana Monsters*, p. 71; Arment and LaGrange, p. 49.
17. Arment and LaGrange, p. 49.
18. "Fisherman lands octopus from Ohio River"; "Indiana man fishing for catfish lands octopus"; "Octopus mystery solved."
19. Arment and LaGrange, p. 51.

Chapter 5

1. Bord and Bord, *Bigfoot Casebook Updated*.
2. Bigfoot Field Researchers Organization (hereafter BFRO); Bord and Bord, *Bigfoot Casebook Updated*; Gulf Coast Bigfoot Research Organization (hereafter GCBRO); International Bigfoot Society (hereafter IBS); KBF.
3. KBF.
4. Faragher, pp. 308-9; IBS No. 2697.
5. Green, p. 222.
6. Ibid., pp. 222-3.
7. Arment, *Historical Bigfoot*, pp. 304-6.
8. Ibid., pp. 304-6.
9. Ibid., p. 161.
10. Bord and Bord, *Bigfoot Casebook Updated*, pp. 22-3, 221; Arment, *Historical Bigfoot*, pp. 161-3.
11. Arment, *Historical Bigfoot*, pp. 163-4.
12. Jewell Castle, letter to the author, August 15, 2007.
13. Green, pp. 65-6.
14. IBS No. 170.
15. IBS No. 170.
16. IBS No. 2829.
17. GCBRO; Nunnelly, *Mysterious Kentucky*, p. 134; John Kleber, *The Encyclopedia of Louisville* (Lexington: University Press of Kentucky, 2001), p. 713.
18. GCBRO; Kleber, *Encyclopedia of Louisville*, p. 713.
19. Creature Chronicles, http://home.cinci.rr.com/kd8afh/kentucky.htm.
20. Bigfoot Encounters; BFRO #5678.
21. BFRO #2155.
22. BFRO #1024; GCBRO; Kentucky Bigfoot.
23. Bigfoot Encounters; Kentucky Bigfoot.
24. GCBRO; KBF.
25. KBF.
26. BFRO #2364; KBF.

27. Bord and Bord, *Bigfoot Casebook Updated*, pp. 233-4; Green, p. 209.
28. GCBRO; Kentucky Bigfoot.
29. Bord and Bord, *Bigfoot Casebook Updated*, pp. 73, 238; Green, p. 223; Keel, pp. 113-14.
30. Bord and Bord, *Bigfoot Casebook Updated*, p. 73; Keel, p. 114.
31. Bord and Bord, *Bigfoot Casebook Updated*, pp. 74, 238; KBF.
32. KBF.
33. Ibid.
34. USA Place Names; GCBRO; Kentucky Bigfoot.
35. Bord and Bord, *Bigfoot Casebook Updated*, p. 252; Green, p. 223.
36. KBF; Nunnelly, *Mysterious Kentucky*, pp. 92-6.
37. KBF.
38. GCBRO; KBF.
39. BFRO #6210.
40. BFRO #2385; IBS #634 and 2984; KBF.
41. BFRO #2390; KBF.
42. BFRO #2428.
43. Coleman and Clark, *Creatures*, pp. 114-16; Bord and Bord, *Bigfoot Casebook Updated*, p. 274; KBF.
44. GCBRO; KBF.
45. BFRO #10765; GCBRO; KBF.
46. KBF.
47. KBF; Nunnelly, *Mysterious Kentucky*, pp. 101-3.
48. KBF; Nunnelly, *Mysterious Kentucky*, pp. 101-3, 109-113; Green, p. 223; Bord and Bord, *Bigfoot Casebook Updated*, p. 285.
49. Bord and Bord, *Bigfoot Casebook Updated*, p. 286; Green, p. 223; KBF.
50. BFRO #2381.
51. GCBRO; USA Place Names.
52. GCBRO; KBF.
53. Bord and Bord, *Bigfoot Casebook Updated*, p. 290; Green, p. 223.
54. BFRO #2430.
55. GCBRO; KBF.
56. KBF; Thompson, "From the Woods."
57. Keith Lawrence, "The Fairview horror," *UFO Report* (May 1979): 70; Bord and Bord, *Bigfoot Casebook Updated*, pp. 302-3.
58. BFRO #912.
59. BFRO #3269.
60. BFRO #2383; KBF.
61. IBS #176; KBF.
62. Bord and Bord, *Bigfoot Casebook Updated*, p. 305; Creature Chronicles; GCBRO; KBF.
63. GCBRO.
64. Bord and Bord, *Bigfoot Casebook Updated*, p. 308; Creature Chronicles; KBF.
65. KBF.
66. BFRO #2425; Bord and Bord, *Bigfoot Casebook Updated*, pp. 169, 309; KBF.
67. Bord and Bord, *Bigfoot Casebook Updated*, pp. 169, 309; BFRO #2382; KBF.
68. BFRO #2426; KBF.
69. BFRO #1850.
70. KBF.
71. Thompson, "Beast of LBL."
72. Nunnelly, *Mysterious Kentucky*, pp. 114-18.
73. GCBRO; Bigfoot Encounters.
74. BFRO #9407; KBF.
75. GCBRO.
76. BFRO #2429; GCBRO; IBS #863; KBF.
77. GCBRO; KBF.
78. KBF.
79. KBF; USA Place Names.
80. KBF.
81. KBF; USA Place Names; BFRO #4624.
82. Thompson, "Forest creature"; BFRO #317.
83. KBF; BFRO #2391.
84. GCBRO; KBF; BFRO #7023.
85. IBS #901, 1095, 2363, 3352, 3863; KBF; BFRO #1045, 2435.
86. GCBRO; BFRO #2435; KBF.
87. BFRO #2384, 2389; KBF.
88. KBF; BFRO #11998, 12641.
89. IBS #2882; BFRO #2367; KBF.
90. BFRO #2367, 3253; Ohio Bigfoot Search Group; KBF; GCBRO.
91. GCBRO; KBF; BFRO #8715.
92. GCBRO; BFRO #1433; Bigfoot Encounters; KBF.
93. BFRO #1265, 10556; KBF; GCBRO.
94. KBF.
95. BFRO #5881; GCBRO.
96. GCBRO; BFRO #6632.
97. BFRO #11966; KBF.
98. KBF.
99. BFRO #8517.
100. KBF.
101. GCBRO.

102. KBF; GCBRO; BFRO #13289.
103. KBF.
104. KBF.
105. KBF.
106. KBF
107. KBF; GCBRO.
108. KBF; USA Place Names; BFRO #24674, 24976.
109. KBF; BFRO #24948, 2527.
110. Arment, Historical Bigfoot, p. 9; Newton, *Encyclopedia of Cryptozoology*, pp. 286, 315, 481-2.
111. Arment, *Historical Bigfoot*, pp. 8, 32.
112. Ibid., pp. 9.
113. Ibid., p. 35; Newton, *Encyclopedia*, p. 307.
114. Myra Shackley, *Still Living?* (New York: Thames & Hudson, 1983), pp. 34-51.
115. Coleman, *Mysterious America*, pp. 206-20; Coleman and Huyghe, *Field Guide to Bigfoot*, pp. 14-17, 20-3, 29-31, 42-3.
116. Coleman, *Mysterious America*, pp. 160-87; Coleman and Huyghe, *Field Guide to Bigfoot*, pp. 34-7, 60-1.

Chapter 6

1. Collins, pp. 209-10.
2. Quoted at RootsWeb, http://newsarch.rootsweb.com/th/read/KYLESLIE/200401/1074324678.
3. Nunnelly, *Mysterious Kentucky*, p. 19; Eberhart, p. 195.
4. Arment, "Giant Amerindians"; Nunnelly, *Mysterious Kentucky*, pp. 19-20.
5. Arment, "Giant Amerindians"; Nunnelly, *Mysterious Kentucky*, pp. 19-20.
6. Smith, pp. 157-8; Nunnelly, *Mysterious Kentucky*, p. 155.
7. Bord and Bord, *Unexplained Mysteries*, pp. 243, 418.
8. Nunnelly, *Mysterious Kentucky*, pp. 158-9.
9. Ibid., pp. 134-5.
10. Ibid., p. 134; Kleber, *The Encyclopedia of Louisville*, p. 713.
11. Quoted in Hall, *Thunderbirds*, pp. 77-8.
12. Hall, *Thunderbirds*, pp. 79-81.
13. Ibid., p. 81.
14. Bord and Bord, *Alien Animals*, p. 129; Coleman, *Mothman*, pp. 173-4.
15. Hall, *Thunderbirds*, p. 81.
16. Ibid., pp. 14-18, 81, 190; Nunnelly, *Mysterious Kentucky*, p. 158.
17. Nunnelly, *Mysterious Kentucky*, pp. 156-8.
18. Ibid., pp. 155-6.
19. Coleman, *Mothman*, p. 26.
20. Nunnelly, *Mysterious Kentucky*, p. 134; KBF.
21. Gooch, Pennyrile, p. 73.
22. Ibid., pp. 74-5.
23. Ibid., p. 74.
24. Ibid., p. 75.
25. Ibid., pp. 73, 75.
26. Ibid., pp. 74-6.
27. Ibid., pp. 77, 79-82.
28. Ibid., pp. 74-5; Kentucky Department of Fish and Wildlife Resources, Species Information.
29. Newton, *Strange Indiana Monsters*, pp. 99-100; Nunnelly, *Mysterious Kentucky*, pp. 119, 125-6; BFRO #3253; KBF.
30. Nunnelly, *Mysterious Kentucky*, pp. 119-20.
31. Thompson, "Beast of LBL"; Nunnelly, *Mysterious Kentucky*, pp. 127-32.
32. Nunnelly, *Mysterious Kentucky*, pp. 121-2.
33. Nunnelly, *Mysterious Kentucky*, pp. 120, 122-5.
34. Coleman, *Mysterious America*, p. 245.
35. Nickell, "Siege."
36. Davis and Bloecher, p. 15.
37. Nickell, "Siege."
38. Ibid.
39. Ibid.
40. Davis and Bloecher, p. 14; Nickell, "Siege."
41. Davis and Bloecher, p. 35; Nickell, "Siege."
42. Coghlan, p. 28.
43. KBF; Nunnelly, *Mysterious Kentucky*, p. 133.
44. KBF; Nunnelly, *Mysterious Kentucky*, p. 133.
45. KBF; Nunnelly, *Mysterious Kentucky*, p. 132.
46. Arment, *Historical Bigfoot*, pp. 304-8; KBF; Nunnelly, *Mysterious Kentucky*, p. 132.
47. KBF; Nunnelly, *Mysterious Kentucky*, pp. 143-6.
48. KBF; Nunnelly, *Mysterious Kentucky*, pp. 146-151.
49. Nunnelly, *Mysterious Kentucky*, pp. 151-3.
50. Thompson, "Creature of the Night"; Nunnelly, *Mysterious Kentucky*, pp. 114-18.
51. Thompson, "Creature of the Night"; Nunnelly, *Mysterious Kentucky*, pp. 114-18.
52. Thompson, "Creature of the Night"; Nunnelly, *Mysterious Kentucky*, pp. 114-18.
53. Nunnelly, *Mysterious Kentucky*, pp. 65-6.
54. Ibid., pp. 66-7.
55. Ibid., pp. 66-7.
56. Ibid., pp. 57-8.
57. Ibid., pp. 58-9.
58. Ibid., p. 59.

59. Duncan, *Living Stories of the Cherokee*, pp. 183-7; Roth, *American Elves*, pp. 29-33.
60. Patton, "Little White Men."
61. Nunnelly, *Mysterious Kentucky*, pp. 61-2.
62. Ibid., pp. 63-5.
63. Ibid., pp. 62-3.
64. Ibid., pp. 60-1.
65. Ibid., p. 139.
66. Ibid., p. 139.
67. Don Wilson DeeAnn and Reeder, *Mammal Species of the World, 3rd edition* (Baltimore: Johns Hopkins University Press, 2005), pp. 532-48.
68. Coleman and Clark, *Cryptozoology A to Z*, pp. 221-4; Walt Williams, "Mystery monster returns home after 121 years." Bozeman (MT) Chronicle, November 15, 2007.
69. USA Place Names.
70. Nunnelly, *Mysterious Kentucky*, p. 143; Newton, *Encylcopedia of Cryptozoology*, pp. 102-5.
71. Nunnelly, *Mysterious Kentucky*, p. 143; "The Haunting of Pine Hill," http://www.geocities.com/pinehill_2003; "Haunted...Westfield's Cemetery?" http://musingsofanoldman.blogspot.com/2006/09/hauntedwestfields-cemetery.html.

Conclusion

1. Newton, *Encyclopedia of Cryptozoology*, pp. 6
2. "Two new monkey species found in Brazil," BBC News, June 25, 2002,
3. "Seven new species found in Bolivia," BBC News, June 24, 2003.
4. Jocelyn Selim, "The list gets longer: New primates found," Discover, http://discovermagazine.com/2005/apr/new-primates-found.
5. Lewis Smith, "Amazon explorers discover 40 new species in a 'lost world' of rainforest," *The Times* (London), September 30, 2006.
6. "Scientists find 24 new species in Suriname," MSNBC, Jne 4, 2007.
7. Lewis Smith, "21 new species found in forest that has kept its secrets since the Ice Age," *The Times* (London), September 26, 2007.
8. Amazon Association for the Preservation of Nature, http://www.marcvanroosmalen.org/index.html.
9. Alice Short, "14 new species found in Brazil," *Los Angeles Times*, April 30, 2008.
10. Kristen Gelineau, "Hundreds of new species found on reefs," *Boston Globe*, September 19, 2008.
11. U.S. Census Bureau, http://quickfacts.census.gov/qfd/states/21000.html; National Park Service Public Use Statistics Office, http://www.nature.nps.gov/stats/state. cfm?st=ky.
12. Bear Research in Kentucky's Central Appalachian Ecosystem; Heald, Barbour and Davis, p. 250.
13. Barbour and Davis, p. 250; Bear Research in Kentucky's Central Appalachian Ecosystem; Heald, "Rising black bear population in Kentucky a good sign."
14. Heald; Administrative Regulation Review Subcommittee Minutes of the December Meeting, http://www.e-archives.ky.gov/Minutes/ legislate/Admin/021210.htm; KDFWR Urges Against Feeding Black Bears; "Kentucky man faces charges for killing bear"; Alford, "Man who killed bear rejects plea bargain"; "Kentucky considering a bear hunting season."
15. David Macdonald, *The Encyclopedia of Mammals* (New York: Facts on File, 1995), p. 446.
16. "Lakes" and "Rivers" in *The Kentucky Encyclopedia*, http://www.kyenc.org.
17. Kentucky Swamps, http://kentucky.hometownlocator.com/features/physical,class,Swamp.cfm.
18. BFRO; GCBRO; IBS; KBF.
19. "Lakes" in *The Kentucky Encyclopedia*.
20. "Ohio River" in *The Kentucky Encyclopedia*.
21. "Licking River" in *The Kentucky Encyclopedia*.
22. "Green River" in *The Kentucky Encyclopedia*.
23. Kentucky Department of Fish and Wildlife Resources, "Snakehead found in west Kentucky"; Dyer, "Piranhas are biting in the Ohio"; "Boy hooks piranha-like fish from Ohio River"; "Rare, tropical fish found in local river"; U.S. Geological Survey, Nonindigenous Aquatic Species.
24. Kentucky Division of Forestry: http://www.forestry.ky.gov/forestfacts; "Forests, Kentucky State," in *The Kentucky Encyclopedia*; U.S. Forest Service, http://www.fs.fed.us/r8/boone.
25. U.S. Forest Service; National Park Service, http://www.nps. gov; Kentucky Division of Forestry.
26. Meldrum, Sasquatch, pp. 137-178.
27. Ibid., pp. 55-72, 251-9.
28. Eberhart, p. 67; Meldrum, pp. 261-70.
29. BFRO #7-23; Bigfoot Encounters; Bord and Bord, *Bigfoot Casebook Updated*, pp. 73-4, 169-70, 284.
30. Arment, Cryptozoology, p. 94.
31. Ichthyology at the Florida Museum of Natural History, http://www.flmnh.ufl.edu/fish/Sharks/Megamouth/mega.htm; Arment, Cryptozoology, pp. 96-8, 122.
32. Arment, *Cryptozoology*, pp. 15, 99-102; Arment, *Boss Snakes*, pp. 12-18.
33. Arment, *Cryptozoology*, pp. 103-6, 108-11.
34. Ibid., pp. 111-15.
35. Ibid., pp. 113-22.
36. Ibid., pp. 343-54; Kentucky Department of Fish and Wildlife Resources.
37. Arment, *Cryptozoology*, pp. 123-4.
38. Ibid., pp. 124-7.

Bibliography

Alford, Roger. "Man who killed bear rejects plea bargain." *Lexington Herald-Leader*, August 25, 2004.
American Wild Boar, www.suwanneeriverranch.com/wild-boar.htm.
"Another piranha caught in Boonville lake." WFIE-TV, Channel 14 (Evansville, Ind.), July 18, 2006.
"Are mountain lions attacking pets in Kentucky?" WFIE-TV, Channel 14 (Evansville, Ind.), June 16, 2004.
Arment, Chad. *Boss Snakes*. Landisville, Pa.: Coachwhip, 2008.
—. *Cryptozoology: Science & Speculation*. Landisville, Pa.: Coachwhip, 2004.
—. "Dinos in the U.S.A." *North American BioFortean Review 2, no. 2* (2000): 32-9.
—. "Giant Amerindians." *North American BioFortean Review 1* (April 1999): 19.
—. *The Historical Bigfoot*. Landisville, Pa.: Coachwhip, 2006.
Arment, Chad, and Brad LaGrange. "A freshwater octopus?" *North American BioFortean Review* 5 (December 2000): 47-51.
Australia Museum Online. "Why most animals are insects," www.amonline.net.au/factsheets/adaptive_radiation.htm.
Barbour, Roger, and Wayne Davis. *Mammals of Kentucky*. Lexington: University Press of Kentucky, 1974.
Bear Research in Kentucky's Central Appalachian Ecosystem, http://www.beartrust.org/KY.html.
Bigfoot Encounters, http://www.bigfootencounters.com.
Bigfoot Field Researchers Organization, www.bfro.net/GDB/state_listing.asp?state=ky.
"Bigfoot spotted in Ohio River valley?" Maysville Kentucky Blog, www.maysvilleexplorer.com/blog/entry.do?blogid=1&entryid=490&entry=2007-2-Bigfoot-Spotted-in-Ohio-River-Valley.
"Black bear sightings becoming more frequent in Kentucky." WKYT-TV, Channel 27 (Lexington, KY), June 22, 2007.
Bord, Janet, and Colin Bord. *Alien Animals*. Harrisburg, PA: Stackpole Books, 1981.
—. *Bigfoot Casebook Updated*. Enumclaw, WA: Pine Winds Press, 2006.
—. *Unexplained Mysteries of the 20th Century*. Chicago: Contemporary Books, 1989.
"Boy hooks piranha-like fish from Ohio River." WLWT-TC, Channel 5 (Cincinnati), June 5, 2007.
Butz, Bob. *Beast of Never, Cat of God*. Guilford, CT: Lyons Press, 2005.
"Canip Monster is sighted again." *Trimble County Banner*, July 31, 1975.
"Captain Chaos gets new home in South Carolina," www.uga.edu/~srel/pr7-18-01.htm.
Clark, Jerome. *Unexplained!* Detroit: Visible Ink, 1993.
—. *Unnatural Phenomena*. Santa Barbara: ABC-CLIO, 2005.
Coghlan, Ronan. *A Dictionary of Cryptozoology*. Bangor, Norther Ireland: Xiphos, 2004.
Coleman, Loren. *Bigfoot! The True Story of Apes in America*. New York: Paraview Pocket Books, 2003.
—. "Mammoth Cave mystery cat sightings." Cryptomundo, www.cryptomundo.com/cryptozoo-news/cave-cougars.
—. *Mothman and Other Curious Encounters*. New York: Paraview Press, 2002.
—. *Mysterious America*. New York: Paraview Press, 2001.
Coleman, Loren, and Jerome Clark. *Cryptozoology A to Z*. New York: Fireside, 1999.
—. *Creatures of the Outer Edge*. New York: Warner, 1978.
Coleman, Loren, and Patrick Huyghe. *The Field Guide to Bigfoot, Yeti, and Other Mystery Primates Worldwide*. New York: Avon, 1999.
—. *The Field Guide to Lake Monsters, Sea Serpents, and Other Mystery Denizens of the Deep*. New York: Tarcher/Penguin, 2003.
Collins, Lewis. *Historical Sketches of Kentucky*. Maysville, KY: Lewis Collins, 1848.
Conant, Roger, and Joseph Collins. *A Field Guide to Reptiles & Amphibians: Eastern and Central North America*, 3rd ed. New York: Houghton Mifflin, 1998.
Cornell University News Service. "Long thought extinct, ivory-billed woodpecker rediscovered in Big Woods of Arkansas," April 28, 2005.
Cox, Lori. "Pets, pests, or simply threats?" *Kentucky Post* (Covington), May 19, 2004.
Crawford, Byron. "Mountain lion makes foray to edge of town." *Courier-Journal*, February 4, 2004.
—. "Mountain lion reports on the rise in 3 counties." *Courier-Journal*, June 18, 2004.
—. "Sightings spur man's search for 'black panther.'" *Courier-Journal*, November 3, 1989.
—. "State wants to know if cougar is back." *Courier-Journal*, July 23, 1980.
Creature Chronicles, http://home.cinci.rr.com/kd8afh.
Davis, Isabel, and Ted Bloecher. *Close Encounter at Kelly and Others of 1955*. Evanston, IL: Center for UFO Studies, 1978.
Dunbar, Lisa. "An alligator never makes a good pet." *Ledger Independent* (Maysville, Ky.), December 15, 2006.
Duncan, Barbara. *Living Stories of the Cherokee*. Chapel Hill: University of North Carolina Press, 1998.
Dyer, Ervin. "Piranhas are biting in the Ohio." *Pittsburgh Post-Gazette*, September 8, 2001.
Eberhart, George. *Mysterious Creatures: A Guide to Cryptozoology*. Santa Barbara: ABC-CLIO, 2002.
Endangered Species in Kentucky, www.endangeredspecies.com/states/ky.htm.
Engeler, Elian. "52 new species discovered on Borneo Island." World Wildlife Fund, December 18, 2006.

Ernst, Carl, and Roger Barbour. *Turtles of the World*. Washington, DC: Smithsonian Institution Press, 1989.
Faragher, John. *Daniel Boone: The Life And Legend of An American Pioneer*. New York: Henry Holt, 1992.
Fenly, Leigh. "In 2006, scientists discovered a whole new world of species." *Union-Tribune* (San Diego), December 28, 2006.
"Fisherman lands octopus from Ohio River." WHAS-TV, Channel 11 (Louisville, Ky.), August 20, 2006.
Ford, Steve. "A lion in our midst?" *Evansville Courier & Press*, June 22, 2008.
Francis, Scott. *Monster Spotter's Guide*. Cincinatti: HOW Books, 2007.
Free Republic, www.freerepublic.com/focus/f-news/1652826/posts.
Garner, Betty. *Monster! Monster!* Blaine, Wash.: Hancock House, 1995.
Gooch, Joe. *The Pennyrile: History, Stories, Legends*. Evansville, IN: Whipporwill, 1982.
Green, John. *Sasquatch: The Apes Among Us*. Blaine, Wash.: Hancock House, 1978.
Gulf Coast Bigfoot Research Organization, www.gcbro. com/kydb1.htm.
Hall, Mark. "Giant snakes in the twentieth century." *Wonders 4* (March 1995): 11-29.
—. *Living Fossils: The Survival of Homo gardarensis, Neandertal Man, and Homo erectus*. Minneapolis: Mark A. Hall Publications, 1999.
—. *Thunderbirds--The Living Legend, 2nd ed*. Minneapolis: Mark A. Hall Publications, 1994.
—. *The Yeti, Bigfoot and True Giants*. Minneapolis: Mark A. Hall Publications, 1997.
Heald, Aimee. "Rising black bear population in Kentucky a good sign." University of Kentucky College of Agriculture, http://www.ca.uky.edu/agc/news/2003/Jul/bears.htm.
"Hunt for escaped alligator called off." *United Press International*, September 8, 2005.
"Indiana man fishing for catfish lands octopus." WLKY-TV, Channel 32 (Louisville, Ky.), August 9, 2006.
"It's some big cat, but is it a cougar?" *Grayson County News-Gazette* (Leitchfield, Ky.), August 26, 2004.
J. Vaughn's Bigfoot/Sasquatch Page, http://www.geocities.com/j_vaughn/bigfoot.html.
Kalman, Matthew. "8 new species found in a cave." *Boston Globe*, June 1, 2006.
Karyl, Anna. *The Kelly Incident*. Vallejo, Calif.: Gateway, 2004.
Keel, John. *The Complete Guide to Mysterious Beings*. New York: Doubleday, 1994.
Kentuckiana Bigfoot and Ariel [sic] Phenomena Research, http://www.barbarianbros.com.
Kentucky Bigfoot, kentuckybigfoot.com.
"Kentucky considering a bear hunting season." *Kentucky Post*, June 22, 2008.
Kentucky Department of Fish and Wildlife Resources. "KDFWR urges against feeding black bears," http://fw.ky. gov/0715c04. asp.
—. "Snakehead found in west Kentucky," http://www.kdfwr.state.ky.us/091405.asp?lid=1250&NavPath=C105C122C44 7.
—. Species Information, http://fw.ky.gov/kfwis/speciesInfo/speciesList.asp?strGroup=1&strSort1=CommonName&strS ort2=ScientificName&strSort3=Class.
The Kentucky Encyclopedia, http://www.kyenc.org.
Kentucky Exotic Pest Plant Council, http://www.se-eppc.org/ky/ index.htm.
"Kentucky man faces charges for killing bear." *Liberty Matters News Service*, http://www.liberty matters.org/newsservice/2004/newsservice08_25_04.htm.
"Kentucky man finds python in rental car." *Boston Globe*, May 29, 2006.
Kentucky Ornithological Society. Reports of Rare Species to the Kentucky Bird Records Committee http://www. biology. eku.edu/KOS/seasonal_reports.htm.
Kentucky Wild Boar, http://www.huntingtripsrus.com/wild-boar-hoghunting/kentucky.html.
Kirk, John. *In the Domain of the Lake Monsters*. Toronto: Key Porter Books, 1998.
"KY black panther." Cryptozoology.com, http://www.cryptozoology.com/sightings/sightings_show.php?id=437.
"Local cougar sightings." The Waterman and Hill-Traveller's [sic] Companion, http://www.naturealmanac.com/cougars/sightings_2004.html.
Mackal, Roy. *Searching for Hidden Animals: An Enquiry into Zoological Mysteries*. Garden City, NY: Doubleday, 1980.
Mandl, Scott. "Man reports sighting wildcat." *Richmond Register*, October 26, 1991.
Mardis, Bill, and Ken Shmidheiser. "Giant gator on Lake Cumberland? Not!!" *Commonwealth Journal* (Somerset, KY), April 28, 2008.
McArthur, David. "Henry County residents spooked by possible cougar sightings." WAVE-TV, Channel 3 (Louisville, KY), June 14, 2004.
Meldrum, Jeff. *Sasquatch: Legend Meets Science*. New York: Tom Doherty, 2006.
"Missing alligator found." WTVF-TV, Channel 5 (Nashville, TN), September 9, 2005.
"Monster still sought." *Trimble County Banner*, August 7, 1975.
"Mountain lion sightings in northern Kentucky." WKRC-TV, Channel 12 (Cincinnati), Jan. 9, 2007.
"Mountain lion on the loose?" WHAS-TV, Channel 11 (Louisville), June 14, 2004.
Music, Mary. "Charges dropped over illegal alligator in store." *Appalachian News Express* (Pikeville, Ky.), June 15, 2007.
National Geographic Field Guide to the Birds of North America 3rd ed. Washington: National Geographic Society, 1999.
"New insect species found in Thailand." *United Press International*, May 24, 2007.
Newton, Michael. *Encyclopedia of Cryptozoology: A Global Guide*. Jefferson, N.C.: McFarland, 2005.
—. *Florida's Unexpected Wildlife*. Gainesville: University Press of Florida, 2007.
—. *Strange Indiana Monsters*. Atglen, Pa.: Schiffer Publishing, 2006.
Nickell, Joe. "Siege of the 'little green men." Skeptical Inquirer, November-December 2006, http://findarticles.com/p/articles/mi_m2843/is_6_30/ai_n16834255.
Nunnelly, B.C. *Mysterious Kentucky*. Decatur, Ill.: Whitechapel Press, 2007.
—. "A Mysterious Kentucky Water Cryptid." *In Cryptozoology and the Investigation of Lesser-Known Mystery Animals*, edited by Chad Arment, pp. 54-8. Landisville, PA: Coachwhip, 2009.
—. Personal correspondence, May 31, 2007.
"Octopus mystery solved." Indianapolis Star, August 10, 2006.
Patton, Donald. "Little White Men in Kentucky." http://www.legendsofamerica.com/GH-KentuckyLittleMen.html.
"Piranha caught in Ohio River." Erie (P.) *Times-News*, May 13, 2002.
Piranha-Fury, <www.piranhafury.com/pfury/index.php?s=2a8749a109dc3a6f08da0ee3f4e075db&showtopic=117961& st=0&p=1426700&#entry1426700.
Place Names. <www.placenames.com/us/12.
"Over 800 new insect species found in Tibet." *People's Daily* (China), May 24, 2000.

Potter, Megan. "Cougars back in Kentucky?" Lexington (KY) *Herald-Leader*, June 8, 2006.

"Rare, tropical fish found in local river." WTOV-TV, Channel 9 (St. Clairsville, Ohio), August 16, 2007.

Rosales, Albert. 1975 Humanoid Reports, http://www. ufoinfo.com/humanoid/humanoid1975.shtml.

Roth, John. *American Elves*. Jefferson, NC: McFarland, 1997.

Sanderson, Ivan. *Abominable Snowmen: Legend Come to Life*. Philadelphia: Chilton Books, 1961.

Shuker, Karl. *Mystery Cats of the World*. London: Robert Hale, 1989.

Smith, Harry. *Fifty Years of Slavery in the United States of America*. Grand Rapids: West Michigan Printing Co., 1891.

Thompson, Jan. "The Beast of LBL," http://www. guardiantales.freewebspace.com/JAN-Beast.html.

—. "Creature of the Night," http://www.guardiantales.freewebspace.com/JAN-Creature.html.

—. "Forest Creature," http://www.guardiantales.freewebspace.com/JAN-Forest.html.

—. "From the woods," http://www.guardiantales. freewebspace.com/JAN-FromTheWoods. html.

University of Kentucky Department of Entomology. Kentucky Critter Files, http://www.uky.edu/Ag/CritterFiles/casefile/casefile.html.

U.S. Department of Agriculture, National Invasive Species Information Center, http;//www.invasivespeciesinfo.gov/animals/ main.shtml.

U.S. Fish and Wildlife Service. "Historic ultralight migration leads majestic whooping cranes over the skies of Kentucky," http://www.fws.gov/southeast/news/2003/r03-127.html.

—. "Snakehead stories." http://www.fws.gov/ snakehead3.htm.

U.S. Geological Survey. Nonindigenous Aquatic Species, nas.er.usgs.gov.

Ward, Joe. "Professor says 'monster' swims in Herrington Lake." *Louisville Courier-Journal*, August 7, 1972.

White, Bob. "Giant alligator in Kentucky lake." *News Enterprise* (Elizabethtown, Ky.), April 13, 2008.

Whitehead, Shelly. "Cougar sightings reported in Kenton County." *Cincinnati Post*, September 19, 2003.

Woolheater, Craig. "Cougar sightings in Kentucky," Cryptomundo, http://www.cryptomundo.com/bigfoot-report/ky-cougar.

Zabarenko, Deborah. "Purple frog among 24 new species found in Suriname." Reuters, June 4, 2007.

Monster Index